HOW *to* LEAP *a* GREAT WALL *in* CHINA

The China Adventures of a
Cross-Cultural Trouble-Shooter

Den Leventhal

To Frances,

祝您健康

Den Leventhal

HOW *to* LEAP *a* GREAT WALL *in* CHINA

The China Adventures of a Cross-Cultural Trouble-Shooter

Den Leventhal

MERWIN
ASIA

An Independent Publisher of Books on East Asia

MERWIN

ASIA

MerwinAsia
59 West St., Unit 3W
Portland, ME 04102
USA

Distributed by the University of Hawai'i Press

Library of Congress Control Number: 2014940129

978-1-937385-58-3 (Paperback)
978-1-937385-59-0 (Hardcover)

Printed in the United States of America

The paper used in this publication meets the minimum
requirements of the American National Standard for Information
Services—Permanence of Paper for Printed Library Materials,
ANSI/NISO Z39/48-1992

Dedicated to the love of my life

Dr. Mary Ward Wilson Leventhal, BSc, MBA, EdD

wife

lover

life partner

best friend

soul mate

mom

nana

teacher

and

really tough editor

Contents

Acknowledgments

My heartfelt thanks are extended to the friends and business colleagues who joined me in living a world of change and exploration in the Greater China region—a journey that began in 1971. Several times throughout the past few years while writing my memoir, I reached out to some of these special people to reconfirm, and ask for elaboration on, the specific experiences that we shared. A. David Dickert and Bjorn Segerblom were particularly helpful in this regard. Thank you. Additional friends and colleagues took time to read various draft iterations of my memoir to provide editorial insights and perspectives. Thank you to Ann Wilson Bierman, Joel Brandes, Professor Jonathan Goldstein, Charles Learner, David Leventhal, Joscelyn Leventhal, Megan Ostwind, and Professor Albert Hoy Yee.

Thank you, too, to Chip Brittingham and Professor Vera Schwarcz who provided not only very useful criticism of the manuscript, but also descriptive and complimentary remarks for publication. In addition, the remarkable and thoughtful Carolyn Brehm, a colleague from my early days in China, was meticulous in her reading of the final draft. She also stimulated further thinking on my part, and I thank Carolyn for writing the book's foreword. Moreover, my publisher Doug Merwin shared his well-grounded experience and expertise to shepherd this book to press. Thank you, Doug.

Finally, three years ago, my loving wife Dr. Mary Wilson Leventhal and I started an electrifying dialogue about cultures that has not finished; and very well might not ever be finished. Coincidentally, as I was writing my memoir, Mary was engaged in her own writing. She was on a scholarly journey to pin down the meaning of intercultural competence. Our life together in East Asia had heightened her commitment to culturally responsive teaching and to tackling how this need could be addressed in the generally monolingual, monocultural teaching force found in American public schools. As she worked at her desk that faced opposite to mine in our home library, we exchanged animated and in-depth conversations on intercultural competence and its role in our contemporary global community. Thank you, Mary, for not only these meaningful discussions, but also for the countless hours of editing and argumentation that made this memoir presentable to the public.

Culture is a continuously evolving creation of mankind . . . and what an amazing mental journey to reflect on what that means in your own life. I had a blast doing just that as I sat at my desk!

Den Leventhal
May 2014

Foreword

Dennis Leventhal is one of America's business pioneers. A scholar of Chinese history, fluent in Mandarin and commanding a deep understanding of Chinese culture and norms, he successfully navigated the nascent China market for several global companies.

His is a story that hasn't been told enough. Reams of books have been written about China's opening to the West and the political ups and downs that have brought the PRC to its place today as the world's second largest economy. Den's story fills a void in "how to do business in China" books by capturing the early days of China's opening to the world. How to Leap is a highly readable and very personal account of how to win in the challenging business culture in the early decades of China's development. Aided by recordings in his China logbook, he weaves a witty and spot-on portrayal of the first generation of American traders who flocked to the PRC in the late 1970s and early 1980s.

Den and I met at the 1980 Fall Canton (Guangzhou) Trade Fair, the semi-annual gathering of Chinese foreign trade corporation representatives and traders from all over the globe that was the exclusive place to conclude contracts in the early years. Den was representing American Cyanamid at the time. It was my second trip to China as a young staffer representing the National Council for US-China Trade, a not-for-profit membership organization established with help from the Nixon White House and the U.S. Congress to facilitate bilateral trade relations. My job was to support the Council's American member companies and report back home on the business that was concluded. We relied on company representatives like Den to share their experiences at a time when we were all learning about this new market.

Over the following two decades, he led several global companies in successful business deals. His road warrior stories are telling. He survived seven banquets in five towns over twelve days, a harrowing river crossing in a rickety boat in between technical seminars, flying "toilet class" on an ancient Russian prop plane, managing home office leaders who created more problems than they solved, and sharing a common love of knot-tying that forged a Chinese business contact into a lifelong friend.

Den's business successes happened before mobile phones or email . . . at a time when long distance phone calls from China needed to be booked a day in advance through the operator.

We can learn a great deal from his story that can be reapplied today. Successful business endeavors start with an understanding of Chinese history, language and culture, along with the ability to form bonds with the people he was doing business with.

China has changed enormously over the past forty years. However, some of the challenges from the early days that Den shares so vividly are still part of the landscape. Petty (and not so petty) corruption, bureaucratic feuding, an inherent disconnect with market demand economics and lack of respect for intellectual property confound American traders and investors today. Den, along with other early entrants to the China market, can take a good deal of credit for contributing to the growth of the Chinese economy and in shaping China's positive perceptions of the West. He succeeded by following ethical business practices and earning the respect and friendship of countless Chinese with whom he did business. There are many lessons here that can be reapplied in 2014.

Carolyn L. Brehm
Vice President, Proctor & Gamble Global
Government Relations & Public Policy
July 2014

HOW *to* LEAP *a* GREAT WALL *in* CHINA

The China Adventures of a
Cross-Cultural Trouble-Shooter

Den Leventhal

Introduction

I blame my seventh grade geography teacher for what happened. She had me draw maps, lots of maps—topographical maps, political maps, historical maps, even climatology maps—for a whole year. After that, I couldn't hear the name of an unfamiliar river, lake, island, desert, mountain chain, isthmus or strait without grabbing the atlas to fix its location in my mind. I believe she made it inevitable that I would make travel to distant places an integral part of my life. Throughout my teen years, I relished examining maps and navigational charts. I read voraciously about explorations around the world—especially those that were related to the seas. I gloried in imagining myself circumnavigating the globe and exploring faraway places. Thus, my geography teacher set my juices in motion for what would follow my public schooling.

A product of what is euphemistically called a lower socio-economic stratum, I managed to gain entrance to the United States Merchant Marine Academy, one of our five federal military service colleges. With infinite gratitude to the American taxpayers who created that opportunity for me, I earned my academic sheepskin, naval reserve officer's commission and mariner's license and was off to see the world. Working as an officer on commercial steamships, I came to navigate not only the oceans of the world but also many cultures of the world.

Seafaring took me many places, but it was my visits to the ports in the Far East that exposed me to unique cultures that had been barely alluded to during my public education. My high school world history course scheduled the discussion of China for the last week of the school year. By then, of course, Asian studies somehow dropped off the curricular horizon due to year-end field trips, proms, final exams and convocations. Thus, my later seafaring experiences in the Far East brought about a keen awareness of cultural dissonance between my own cultural identity as an American and the cultures of Asian peoples.

During our docking, cargo operations, and other such normal transactions between ship and shore in East Asian countries, I observed that intercultural misunderstanding was a seriously limiting factor in getting work done in a timely, safe and effective manner. In fact, it was readily apparent through my observations of numerous cross-cultural interactions that communication difficulties were not limited to linguistic differences. People "out there" perceived things differently, understood the world differently, and reacted to situations differently. They also had differing agendas.

A desire to comprehend what I had experienced eventually thrust me into an Asian Studies graduate program at the University of Pennsylvania. Four years of focus on Chinese history, economics, art, literature, foreign relations, philosophy, religion, language and culture provided me with insights and perspectives that I was eager to explore further. Fortunately, upon my completion of the four-year graduate program, my professors helped me obtain a fellowship to attend the Stanford Chinese Language Center situated at National Taiwan University in Taipei, Taiwan. The Stanford program enabled graduate students to polish their Chinese speaking and reading skills. Now I would be off to Taiwan for a year of advanced Chinese language training and the opportunity to experiment with interacting effectively with the Asian world.

At least, it was supposed to be a one-year sojourn in Taipei.

Much to my surprise and that of my wife Mary, one year stretched into a lifetime career. We shared over thirty years of living among, and working with, Chinese people—first in Taiwan, then in Hong Kong and throughout the Peoples Republic of China (PRC). My business career took me to sixty-two Chinese cities, as well as many other countries, in the process.

Informed by my academic work, I set out on a career in China business development that centered on the importance and value of intercultural understanding. I acquired culturally responsive business strategies that enabled me to spot and handle the proverbial red flags that signal risks and dangers in the affairs of the world. Trouble-shooting these difficulties within a cross-cultural framework evolved into an ongoing, hard-knocks education on doing business in China. Nonetheless, the rigor of my formal Chinese studies framed my multicultural thinking for the achievement of China market entry strategies and problem-solving tactics in the service of transnational corporations. Starting with cross-cultural engagement, I struggled up a steep learning curve to an intercultural understanding that resulted in substantive commercial achievement.

My objective here is to elucidate some of the lessons I've learned as a "shirtsleeve sinologist." Much of what I describe was noted in my twelve-volume hand-written log of my business travel activities from 1980 to 1998—maintaining a logbook was a habit from my seafaring experiences. In the following pages, I describe the problems and peculiarities in cross-cultural communication and intercultural cooperation with the Chinese over the course of my career. Facing a Chinese government monopoly, and developing the strategy and tactics for leaping that virtual Great Wall was a career highlight. I hope that my experiences might prove to be of some instructive value — as well as provide some mild amusement.

Chapter I

Discovering a New Career,
or
How to Solve a Chinese Tax Problem

*—in which I learn that knowledge of Chinese tax law
and company accounting records
are not necessarily required.*

Following a year of intensive Chinese-language training in Taiwan in the early '70s, I decided to stay there to continue private study in the Chinese Classics. I also needed to acquire a livelihood to support my decision to spend another year studying classical Chinese literature and philosophy. So, I grabbed an opportunity to work for a Chinese advertising and public relations agency. That second decision changed the trajectory of my life.

The agency's president and general manager, Mr. Peter Yi-chih Liu, was planning to expand his business. Mr. Liu wanted to go after the advertising accounts of the Taiwan subsidiaries of transnational companies. He sought the assistance of a Westerner who could function in both English and Chinese. I filled the bill. This proved to be my first onsite experience with cross-cultural trouble-shooting in East Asia. My role in Mr. Liu's business expansion plan was to work with the local marketing aspects of such companies as Eastman Kodak and Bristol-Myers.

My responsibilities involved helping Chinese account management teams to analyze the marketing needs of selected targets and develop advertising proposals. I then helped translate the proposals into English, and ofttimes engaged in lively debates over the Chinese naming of a particular product so that both the Chinese and English renditions were attractive. There were two other principal aspects of my working brief. I drilled the account management teams in making polished sales presentations, and I provided counsel on the social cultivation of the Western (usually American) general managers of these subsidiary companies. This latter aspect resulted in my developing a close working relationship with Mr. Liu.

Peter Liu provided my first insight into a not uncommon type of Chinese businessman, i.e., someone who takes pride and pleasure in his own rich cultural tradition. One of Mr. Liu's more noteworthy scholarly achievements was the recovery of Song dynasty period (960–1279 CE) musical compositions for the traditional *guzheng*. The *guzheng* is a zither-like thirteen-stringed instrument. In fact, he played the *guzheng* expertly, and included time to enjoy this instrument as part of his daily regimen. Thus, during the course of my six years working for this Chinese company, I got to know Peter Liu as more than a businessman.

Mr. Liu was a scholar of classical Chinese music, and a full professor of that subject at Tung Hai University in Taichung, the *provincial* capital of Taiwan. Our company staff meetings and luncheon meetings frequently wandered off course to discussions of medieval Chinese literature, art, philosophy and society, in addition to music, of course. It was rather satisfying for me not only to be able to contribute substantively to these chats, but also to do so in the Chinese language. One day this facet of my academic training in Chinese studies led to an unusual business assignment.

The unique assignment arrived after I had logged a few years on this job. Peter called me into his office to give me instructions. He wanted me to go to the Tax Office in the Taipei Municipal Government buildings and meet with a particular tax official. Apparently, Peter had received a notice about a corporate tax problem, and the official concerned wanted to meet with a company representative to discuss the matter. This was indeed a special assignment given that my purview was market development. For the life of me I couldn't see a connection between my work in marketing and discussion of a tax problem.

While willing to do anything to help, I felt honor bound to inform my boss that when it came to accounting matters, I couldn't count my way through a Kleenex tissue box. Moreover, I stated the obvious: all my experience was on the marketing side of the business. Continuing to be perplexed as to why Peter would identify the sole Westerner in his company to work with Taiwan Government tax officials, I suggested that the company accountant might be better equipped to deal with the matter.

My suggestion for dealing with the as-yet-unexplained tax problem was met with a chuckle. Peter was adamant in his view that I could handle the situation. Upon my request for a briefing on the nature of the problem, and perhaps some guidance on how best to deal with it, Peter chuckled again. "Actually, all we have is a notice summoning a company representative to discuss some concerns, which were not explained in the note." He advised, "Just go and meet the guy. And, be sure to note the artwork he has under glass on the shelf behind his desk."

With this enigmatic instruction, I went to the meeting. The *objet d'art* that Peter mentioned jumped right out at me. Even a first year art history major would recognize Song period *celadon* ceramics. Peter's gambit became obvious at once. My comment on the pale green crackleware bowl evoked a smile and an hour-long conversation on the evolution of glazing technology and related arcane artistic curiosities within the Chinese historical experience. Medieval Chinese art history had given us a connection.

I could no longer bear the tension of awaiting the exposure of a tax matter that I would assuredly not comprehend. Making friendly conversation was one thing, but solving Peter's problem, whatever it was, was another. The passage of an hour's time and a lull in the conversation gave me the impetus to raise the question. "If I may ask a question, the official notice requesting this meeting did not clarify the nature of this office's concern . . . Could you . . . um . . . "

Without a word to me, he held up a hand. Then, with the dignified air of government authority, the tax bureaucrat opened a ledger. He made an elaborately ceremonious notation in the margins of the page, and smiled. Looking up at me, he smiled once more and stated simply, "The problem is resolved."

When I reported back to my boss, he chuckled and nodded as if the result was not unforeseen. Further reflection suggested to me that Peter had seen the effect a young Chinese-speaking Westerner with an in-depth knowledge of China's cultural history would have on a minor Chinese functionary who had a passion for his own traditions. The so-called problem apparently had nothing to do with taxes. I supposed it was, rather, a matter of showing respect. I never did learn the real motivation for the request for a meeting. I did learn, however, that this not uncommon type of businessman found in Peter Liu was a touchstone for successful business transactions in Chinese culture.

This was the first of many lessons demonstrating that the capacity to connect with Chinese people within their own cultural framework enabled relationships of mutual respect and trust to be built very quickly. This lesson proved applicable in all manner of situations throughout my subsequent career. Quite frankly, anyone who has taken the time and effort to obtain more than a superficial understanding of another culture has gone beyond respect to esteem for that culture. The Chinese appreciate this.

Over the years I've met many Chinese in governmental and business positions of responsibility who were quite knowledgeable about their own history and higher culture. This advantage of having shared interests gave me an edge in dealing with all kinds of problems. At the same time, it is obvious that understanding a foreign language facilitates understanding another's culture. Cultural understandings and worldview are embedded in the syntax and vocabulary of language. The ability to speak Mandarin served as a gateway to demonstrate appreciation for the heritage of those with whom I was doing business.

This particular encounter in the 1970s gave me the first glimmer of an idea for a unique career. Leavened with the historical happenstance of Nixon and Kissinger's opening of the PRC to the U.S.A., my experience with the tax problem marked the beginning of my professional career as a "shirtsleeve sinologist." A capacity for intercultural competence, going beyond the mere ability to converse in the Chinese language, might enable me to generate mutual respect, appreciation and trust. That would make meaningful and productive cooperation on a practical level possible. It was worth a try . . .

Chapter II

The Serendipity Factor,
or
A Chinese Poem Is Worth a Cool Coupla' Million

—in which I develop a unique sales technique
*in a **hard sell** situation.*

There can be no doubt about the usefulness of knowing the language of the country in which you are working. I was most grateful for having that capability when trying to find a usable toilet a mile or so outside of Fushun, a coal-mining town in Liaoning Province, back in the early 1980s. And, in the case of China at least, the local people are always delighted when they meet a foreigner who has made the effort to learn some of their language. No matter how little you know, it's your attempt to communicate on their terms that warms their hearts toward you.

But, language is a funny thing. There are not only many different languages *outside* your own cultural framework, but also there are a number of specialized languages *inside* any one particular language. This was brought home to me during my first few trips to the China mainland.

Early in 1980, one of America's Fortune 500 companies, American Cyanamid Company, threw me into the PRC for the purpose of managing the "dance-cards" of a number of market exploration expeditions. The choreography of the first three delegations from this American manufacturer of specialty chemicals and pharmaceuticals concerned diverse product areas. These included herbicides, pigment production equipment, and surgical supplies. Getting delegations into China was enabled by diplomatic relations between the U.S.A. and the PRC that had been established officially in 1979. Navigating the terrain once inside China could be another matter entirely. The need to exhibit political correctness *a la Chinoise* with all contacts was a veritable minefield. Regulatory structures were a sliding reality built on shifting sands. Market intelligence work was blocked by a state secrets act that covered all aspects of Chinese life like a legal Great Wall. Thus, setting successful market exploration in motion was dependent on how an outside corporate delegation worked within this bevy of factors.

In the summer of 1980, cross-cultural communications were at the fore. I was leading my fourth group of visiting business associates. This group was looking for industrial consumers of chemical additives for plastics. With two chemical engineers in tow, I set up visits to a number of manufacturing plants and their related business management units. All of the units were governmental institutions at the earliest stages of China's evolution toward a market economy. To facilitate relationship building, I always mapped local institutional relationships. In that way, we could estimate who were decision-influencers and who were decision-makers within China's chemicals industry. Mapping institutional relationships was an important tool to make sure productive communication happened during these cross-cultural situations.

For this delegation, institutional mapping was critical if successful communication were to take place. In Shanghai, we first met with representatives of the Municipal Foreign Trade Department—called a "corporation" on the business cards they handed out to foreigners. We then visited a plastic products research institute and several plastics production plants under the auspices of the Jinshan General Petrochemical Corporation. We also had meetings with some other plastics production units that were directly under the control of the Shanghai Municipal Chemical Industry Bureau. The rivalry between the various units was palpable, and created occasional diplomatic problems with our scheduling. Each wanted to control access to these "foreign experts."

Our team quickly came to realize there was a fundamental difference in our respective *business* cultures. Our technical marketing pitch was geared to emphasizing how the stuff we were selling would improve the quality and sales of their end products. This approach assumed that any manufacturing unit was primarily concerned with making a profit by increasing sales. Our assumptions were based on the principles of demand-side economics, *i.e.*, find out what your customers want, and give it to them.

However, our Chinese counterparts were operating with a mentality created by central government dictates, which valued production for its own sake. Since the government provided the consumers, business managers had traditionally no exposure to scoping out markets and sales promotion work. The managers, therefore, were focused primarily on controlling production costs as part of meeting state-dictated production quotas. An historical hangover from traditional Chinese Communist Party (CCP) ideology, theirs was a supply-side mentality.

Our next stop, in Beijing, exemplified this clash of economic orientations. We visited the Yanshan General Petrochemical Works, located 53 km southwest of the Chinese capital. Back then, Yanshan was already a large manufacturing complex, with various units producing ethylene, polypropylene, synthetic rubber, phenol, detergents, and polystyrene. Their annual export sales earnings had already reached US$70 million. Occupying around 36 sq. km., the complex had some 33,000 employees and housed over 80,000 people, including workers' families and foreign technical specialists of various nationalities. As a state-owned manufacturing institution, the complex included residential dwellings, cafeterias, hospitals, and schools, as well as the various production and research units. It was a traditional *iron rice bowl* facility.

This China of their determinedly communist period was

referred to by PRC leaders as a "socialist workers' paradise." Young people were placed in a production unit for life. The unit would provide all their necessities, including food, clothing, shelter, education, and medical care. Choice was not an option. However, their rice bowl, a symbol of each person's basic needs, was said to be made of iron, and therefore could never be broken. They supposedly had a secure lifetime livelihood. As a member of the business delegations visiting this socialist workers' paradise, I had many opportunities to observe the effect of this PRC mindset on business development initiatives between East and West.

For example, for this particular delegation, our five-day visit was filled with plant tours, seminars, technical discussions, lengthy meals, and local cultural tours. It is important to note that cultural tours are not a simple nicety added to the mix of doing business in China. Such tours are a vital component of a delegation's market entry initiative. While working on the Yanshan plastics additives sales project, our delegation was located around 10 km from the caves at Zhoukoudian, where the material remains of the 400,000-year- old *Sinanthropus pekinensis* (*aka* Peking Man) were discovered in 1927. In addition to a short stop there, we also traversed the Marco Polo Bridge—originally constructed in 1189 CE. This bridge was also the site of a Japanese-manufactured "incident" in 1937 that initiated eight years of warfare between China and Japan. Being escorted to local historical sites would turn out to be a hallmark of my travels throughout China during the next two-plus decades. They provided forums for cultivating business associates in the way that golf courses are used for putting together American business deals. The fun of these forays into Chinese historical and scenic sites was counter-balanced by the concern to achieve the business objectives of each of our visiting delegations. Thus, the objective for this delegation was always top of mind regardless of whether the delegation was in formal meetings or otherwise engaged during the China visit.

At Yanshan, one of our marketing objectives was to sell a chemical additive—an ultra-violet light absorber called "UV531." This gunk was designed to reduce effectively the increasing brittleness of chemical polymer products caused by the sun's ultra-violet rays. (It's the ultra-violet light absorber in your kayak's synthetic fiberglass hull that prevents it from breaking up when you slam onto a rock when running the rapids on the Colorado River.) The good news about our UV531 chemical was that it was an excellent product to market to our potential Chinese customers.

But we had a fundamental problem. The chemical goop we were selling was a *me-too* product. That means they were already using a similar additive produced by other companies from other countries. Normally, in this situation, everything boiled down to price for the Chinese, and our market information indicated that our competition was a bit cheaper. After all the talk, conferring, exchanges of protocols, and social niceties, my bottom line was how to address the price issue. Unfortunately, I had no leeway for negotiation on this point from our home office back in the States. I had to find a strategy that would provide another hook to get the Chinese to buy into our product.

Meanwhile, given that I understood very little about chemistry, a considerable portion of my days and nights throughout the trip was focused on picking up sufficient new vocabulary—in both languages—to follow the technical discussions. This involved continuous, intense usage of an English-Chinese chemical engineering dictionary. This aspect of doing business in China was complicated still further. At that time, there was the not unusual occurrence of no agreed upon translation of various commonplace Western *commercial* concepts in the vocabulary of the *socialist workers' paradise*. Thus, I was juggling the development of a successful pricing strategy amid personal struggles at gaining familiarity with new technical jargon and honing effective communications with PRC counterparts who did not yet grasp Western commercial vocabulary.

It was during these first several business trips into the China mainland that I began to perceive that the quality of the interpreters available to us was variable, to say the least. It wasn't merely limits in linguistic capabilities. Nor was it simply ambiguous commercial terminology. Many misinterpretations resulted from differing preconceptions and notions about the objectives, concerns, and agendas of the respective parties. The need for my attention to these critical elements necessitated putting the pricing problem on the mental back burner. Immediately pressing issues arose especially when these chemically savvy people got near a blackboard and chalk. They began to communicate rapidly through the symbols and equations of their mutual technical specialty. Chemistry itself was their common language. This unique linguistic path left us non-technical types in the dust, and led to yet another problem.

Collegial scientific and technical communication was a problem that would plague many foreign companies in the ensuing formative years of China's integration with international business. Specifically, some foreign technical experts had a tendency to "give away the store" in their enthusiasm for communicating with their Chinese technical equals. Through the common language of chemical symbols and formulas, they were euphoric at not being dependent upon a translator to communicate with their Chinese counterparts. The proprietary, and therefore confidential, aspects of their technical knowledge would often be exposed in the enthusiasm of the moment. In this particular case, I observed that while my crew was explaining the chemical effects of our additive, the Chinese technical staff was asking about the recipe for creating its chemical properties. More specifically, they wanted to know how to make our product, and were not bashful about asking for what our home office would consider proprietary information.

The Western businessman understands that his company's proprietary information is not merely a high cost investment in

Research & Development, but also a valuable tool for generating sales of either product or technology. Proprietary information needs to be protected from unlicensed usage. While most technical specialists understand this point, they easily lapse into collegial rapport with fellow scientists and technical experts. Fortunately, most corporate scientists and technicians merely need to be reminded to curb their enthusiasms and sidestep questions of a sensitive nature. The trick for the China market "point man," *i.e.*, me, was to spot the problem when it popped up.

This fundamental understanding stood in direct conflict with the Chinese lack of comprehension with regard to the concept of intellectual property. Socialist ideology asked how mere knowledge of a particular molecular structure could be a commodity in and of itself. Their struggle with this aspect of international commerce is reflected in the difficulties they had in the creation of their own commercial law system. They started in the '80s with a patent law, then created a trademark law, and later added legal protection for service marks. The service mark, i.e., company logo, printed on an inspection report from an internationally recognized inspection services company, such as SGS, is accepted in any court as valid evidence during a legal dispute. It needs to be protected from forgeries.

During this complex, agonizing process, which took around two decades, the leaders of many transnational businesses beat a path to Chinese governmental leaders in Beijing. Transnational companies sought to persuade Chinese lawmakers to do what was necessary to ensure the sanctity of proprietary knowledge. This problem is still not totally resolved, as indicated by the continuing concerns over China's enforcement of Intellectual Property Rights within the context of World Trade Organization (WTO) requirements.

With the price problem of our plastics additive product still nagging at the back of my brain, my marketing function was at the fore during the more social occasions of our business visits. This included cultural tours, sightseeing, and mealtimes. Given a society wherein establishing a basis for trust and viable relationships generally precedes discussion of concrete issues common to most Asian cultures, my job was to generate an atmosphere of comfort, and hopefully trust, with those who headed their business affairs. The many decades of colonial and imperial aggression prior to the founding of the PRC created an historical hangover among many Chinese. That hangover is marked by a subcutaneous xenophobia that could erupt like a nasty rash at the slightest possible cause for distrust. Casual conversations during these breaks in the working program helped to ease unspoken concerns about the trustworthiness of Westerners.

To address this issue, I decided early on that I would work as much as possible directly in Chinese. This necessitated assuring my entourage that I would provide translations of anything of significance mentioned during mealtimes. They seemed to like this approach because it allowed them to focus on a more primal cultural experience, *i.e.,* the food. Thus, I employed this method for our *thank you* banquet near the end of our visit to Yanshan. Most of the staff that had participated in the technically substantive portion of our activities, along with the business manager of the plastics plant, was present. However, our primary guest was one of the several deputy general managers of the entire petrochemical complex. My communicating directly in Chinese would hopefully build the necessary rapport with him for a chance to achieve a successful conclusion to our marketing efforts.

After the drinks were poured and the formal complimentary speeches completed, we got down to the more serious business of eating some twelve courses of Chinese food. At this point, I overheard the plant manager comment in Chinese to the deputy general manager, "Their UV light absorber is the same as the French stuff, but it's almost a penny per kilo more expensive."

An unsavory thought raced through my brain upon hearing his aside to our primary guest: "Given the massive tonnage involved with a standard sized shipment, that would be a lot of pennies!" But since I had only the words I just heard for the price of the French gunk, and he knew that I understood Chinese, I couldn't be sure our price was truly out of the running. His comment may have been a ploy to soften our position on pricing.

Nevertheless, it seemed we were dead in the water at that point. But I plunged ahead anyway. I began by throwing out a few questions about where the deputy general manager came from originally. In China, a question about origins usually refers to one's ancestral home. This enabled me to make some fairly intelligent comments about some historical events well known to the Chinese that had occurred in his native region. His pleasure that a foreigner knew something about Chinese history was open and honest. What followed was a chat that departed completely from the realm of chemistry, plastics, and the economics of supply-and-demand.

Our enthusiastic exchange was accompanied by much toasting with *maotai*. Maotai is the Chinese version of *white lightning* and is made from edible sorghum and an assortment of several other grains—sometimes exceeding 120 proof. By the time our conversation worked its way back to the Tang dynasty (618–906 CE), neither of us was feeling any pain—as the saying goes. At that point, my new "old friend," the deputy general manager, threw out a challenge that made the business manager blanch.

Perhaps I should note here that the DGM was not too checked out in the chemistry relevant to the business deal we were pursuing. In fact, he was an old Party member whose position, as near as I could figure, was based on the fact that he was one of Chairman Mao's troopers. He had participated in the epic Long March of 1934–35, a heroic 6,000-mile trek that saved the Red Army from extinction. On the other hand, this DGM really knew his history! His challenge was a straightforward deal maker-or-breaker. He first expressed pleasure in meeting a young American who knew so much about Chinese history and culture. He then proposed, "I shall now intone a famous poem. I want you to tell me who wrote it. Also, I want you to explain its meaning in English. My interpreter here will tell me if you are correct. If you can do that, we will buy your UV-531 at the autumn Canton Trade Fair."

His business manager said something that sounded like a cross between a hiccup and a gurgle.

Thinking, "What have I got to lose?" I agreed.

At this juncture, you need to understand a few points about classical Chinese poetry. Identifying which period a poem comes from is not too awfully difficult because each major dynastic period had fairly distinctive characteristics in basic form. Basic form entails number of characters per line, number of lines, and stylistic language. However, picking the creator of a particular Chinese language poem is virtually impossible for someone, especially a foreigner, who hasn't devoted years of study to the subject. And as for translating . . .?!! Yeesh!

The scholars, writers, and poets of China's imperial period wrote primarily for an erudite audience. Their audience of the educated elite of China was well versed in their own literary tradition. As a result, they didn't footnote any of their literary references. It was assumed that their readership would have no difficulty recognizing phrases borrowed from the extensive body of literature that served as the foundation and embodiment of Chinese culture. In fact, their compositions were rife with un-annotated allusions to historical texts, philosophical treatises, and even other poetry. Some lines in a poem would *denote* meanings that superficially diverged widely from the poem's primary thematic content, but would enhance the poesy through connotative subtleties.

Like I said, "What did I have to lose?"

The deputy general manager proceeded to recite from memory what was obviously a favorite poem. He gave it a lilting sound vaguely reminiscent of the Peking operatic style and seemed delighted to have the opportunity of making a public performance.

Here's where luck kicked in, *i.e.,* the serendipity factor.

Years earlier, during my graduate studies at UPenn, I was given an assignment to study one Chinese poem. The overt objective was to create a reasonably accurate translation. However, the primary purpose of this exercise was to utilize a number of different research tools to identify the unmarked quotations from other texts in the poem. It was actually a lesson in Chinese historiographical research techniques.

I worked on that dang poem for two months. After my third try at translating it, my professor said, "Okay. Stop . . . ! You're not big on poetry, are you?"

The DGM was reciting that very same poem. And, I had just enough liquid inspiration in me to remember my miserable attempt at translation. You might even say it was a poetic victory because the poet was the Tang dynasty genius Li Bo (710–762), who was a noted lover of fermented juices. In fact, he died of overindulgence in drink, which caused him to fall off a cliff into the Yangzi River and drown. Unlike Li Bo and with hearty, playful good humor, I reveled in this infinitesimally unexpected opportunity to respond to a poem with which I was familiar.

Needless to say, I nailed it! My translation was passable for the Yanshan boss man. And, the deputy general manager instructed me to meet his representative at the next Canton Trade Fair with a draft sales contract in hand, ready to thrash out product specs and shipping details. He kept his word. Our first sale was for a half million U.S. dollars, despite the plant manager's assertion that we were not price competitive with the French manufacturer.

Over the next few years, an occasional social call at Yanshan was sufficient to ensure continued sales, with the final tally exceeding two million dollars.

And, I gained a new appreciation for Chinese poetry . . . Or rather, for one particular Chinese poem.

These experiences reinforced my perception that taking the time to develop a rapport with my Chinese contacts was far more valuable than debating the relative merits of supply-side and demand-side economics. The Chinese would eventually figure out that argument themselves as they developed their own market economy.

Chapter III

The Culture-Bound Mindset,
or
The Ability to Use Chopsticks Doesn't Make
You a China Business Expert

—in which I explore the handling of cross-cultural problem solving.

The two decades following the exchange of ambassadors between Beijing and Washington in 1979 involved great adjustments in governmental and societal perceptions during the period of China's "Opening to the West." There was tremendous dissonance between the values of Chinese socialism and Western democratic capitalism. Social anthropologists refer to *cultural relativism* when they talk about the presupposition that one culture regards itself as inherently superior to others. In this case, both China and America saw themselves as having inherently superior cultures. The Chinese see themselves as members of an ancient civilization built on a solid moral foundation. On the other hand, the American sense of rugged individualism is manifested in self-confidence when handling every conceivable practical problem. These two differing self-perceptions could clash, causing deep-seated obstructions to comprehending how each perceived the other's world. The resultant misunderstandings created problems as each culture attempted to find ways to work cooperatively in productive enterprises.

As the leaders of American-based transnational corporations stirred themselves to see how to approach this new potential market, one of their questions involved finding a workable tactical methodology for spearheading a market entry strategy. Some hired consulting firms that had an Asian focus. Some handed the China market responsibility to their East Asian regional headquarters. Some allowed their home-based senior corporate division executives to figure it out for themselves for their respective business units. Some hired Hong Kong trading companies to serve as their China market "agents." Some set up a cold call China tour for their CEO and his entourage of senior executives. This latter strategy aimed to make high-level Chinese governmental connections that would facilitate the establishment of a corporate foothold of an ill-defined sort. Usually the market entry approach would evolve into a mix of these various methods.

One of the most popular approaches involved hiring a Chinese person, usually a Hong Kong native, and setting him loose to find commercially relevant connections inside China. This approach would purportedly open up access to industrial and commercial organizations of relevance to the transnational corporation's business interests. Given that the two *official* languages in Hong Kong were Cantonese and English, it was generally thought that a local native would be the perfect intermediary for developing the China market for the foreign firm. However, not only is the Cantonese spoken language distinctly different from the Mandarin spoken language, salient cultural differences exist as well between those whose first language is Cantonese and those whose first language is Mandarin. Few Westerners recognized the significant cultural differences between Chinese ethnicities in Hong Kong and in the PRC. Some corporate decision-makers were not aware that the Mandarin dialect of Chinese was the official language of the PRC. Mandarin was taught in all mainland schools, but was rarely part of Hong Kong's public curriculum. Of course, this situation began to change closer to 1997 when China would regain control of Hong Kong from the British.

Those who went the route of appointing their market entry point man based on his Chinese race did not seem to understand some of the wrinkles within Chinese culture. Culturally, regional prejudices exist just as one might expect when comparing, say, New England with the southern states of the United States. Generally speaking, Shanghai people have traditionally regarded themselves as the inheritors of Shanghai's pre-WWII position. That is, they have regarded Shanghai as the center of East Asian commerce, and they resented Hong Kong's contemporary preeminence in that regard. Similarly, the native Cantonese of the region centered on Guangzhou (*aka* Canton) in southern China valued their familial connections with the majority Cantonese population of Hong Kong, but were jealous of the latter's wealth and freedom. Regardless, in general, neither region was culturally responsive to Beijing's northern politically correct way of life.

And, Beijing, well, they relished their contempt for the politically incorrect Southerners in Hong Kong who benefited from what they deemed to be capitalist corruption. I will never forget the first time a Northerner told me a joke about the Southerners. We had been discussing culinary differences within China's various cultural regions. He referred to the Cantonese capacity to find a way to cook and eat anything and everything that walked, wriggled, crawled, swam or flew on the planet. My Beijing friend suddenly chuckled and continued, "Do you know why the Cantonese do not eat submarines?" I replied, "No, why not?" He laughed again and explained, "Because they can't catch them."

It should also be noted that many Chinese equal or even surpass the British when it comes to what is often perceived as linguistic snobbery by Americans. The highest standard in speech is set by the Mandarin spoken in Beijing. As one moves outward from that hub of political correctness, one passes through various regions with numerous variations in Mandarin accent due to local *patois* and regional dialects, arriving eventually in southern China where Cantonese is virtually a different language. Furthermore, most of the Hong Kong Chinese who had learned some Mandarin at that time spoke it with a pronunciation that was somewhat difficult to comprehend. Evidently, to a Northern Chinese, that's about as déclassé as you can get. In fact, the highest compliment I ever received regarding my command of Mandarin illustrates this point. A senior PRC official opined, "When I first spoke with you on the phone, I thought you were from Hebei Province." With unabashed pride, I might mention that region is contiguous to Beijing Municipality.

Add *guanxi* to this communications mix. This is the glue in Chinese society. Loosely translated as "relationships" or "connections," *guanxi* delineates the spider web of tracks upon which individuals move within their own world. This complex of human relationships defines the individual in terms by which each person is responsible for upholding the traditional societal ideal of harmony. This concept of relational hierarchy reinforces behavioral expectations. There are varying social obligations between and among individuals. Evidence of defined social expectations is found in the dim recesses of history subsequent to the canonization of the great philosophical and literary classics of China, *e.g.*, the *Sishu Wujing* (the "Four Books and Five Classics"). These records of social expectations expose the core culture of the Chinese in the way that the *Torah* and the *Talmud* are repositories of the foundational elements of Jewish cultural traditions. Forming what became the Confucian Canon, the majority of these revered texts dealt with rites, rituals and ceremonies which encapsulated an idealized societal political and moral structure. Thus, *guanxi* defines each personal relationship with its requisite set of responsibilities between two people, and in society at large.

An individual's *guanxi* is created by his concrete position within a specific network of family, friends, schools, and work. That network defines who he is as a human being. Violation of this principle of social existence is more than a criminal act; it is self-extinction of the individual. Thus, his capacity to operate outside those circumscribed relationships has to be channeled through other individuals within his own social network. The network of relationships of these other individuals effectively becomes a part of the latter's extended network. Therefore, whenever a local Chinese was interviewing to serve as an agent of a foreign business entity, it was inevitable that he would describe part of his qualifications in terms of his societal connections. You could hear, for example, something like "My auntie's husband's cousin was in the same university class with the nephew of Prime Minister Deng Xiao-ping's grandson's wife's father." The implication would be that the interviewee was thus able to access high level decision-makers within the ruling class through this extended *guanxi* network. Nonetheless, having even the best of *guanxi* may not be of value if there is an absence of cross-cultural understanding in the foreign company's market development executive.

While the market entry point man of Chinese ethnicity grew up with chopsticks, he didn't necessarily understand the *knife and fork* cultural framework. This is where a commercial strategy has to have some unique capabilities. Effective communication is dependent upon intercultural understandings. For successful negotiations, a company's point man must be conversant in the duality of his employer's corporate culture and the culture of the targeted Chinese entity. Having relationships that connect to people on one side of the deal-making equation is one small part of brokering a mutually agreed commercial contract. Let me metaphorically explicate this with a modern fable of a fish and a diver.

Picture an oceanic mining vessel in search of a stash of mineral nodules that normally accumulate in obscure locations on the ocean floor. While the vessel contains electronic probing devices, let's suppose that the vessel's technology does not yet always penetrate to the depths where such lucrative stashes can be found. So, the people running the vessel think, "Let's employ a fish to do some deep probing. A fish is comfortable in that watery environment, and can go where we cannot."

So, they hire a fish. This fish grew up in a school of similar fish. This fish learned from his school of fish which thermal layers to seek, and what underwater currents to follow, to find the food that they traditionally look for in the food chain. The fish also learned to identify his predators, and to observe other underwater creatures that live tangentially to his activity circles. That's his *guanxi* network. However, not only can he not break out of that network, he has not yet learned how to communicate effectively with the mother ship. His understanding of his environment is complete, but intuitive and uncritical. And, that environment is circumscribed by the habits and habitat of his *school*. More importantly, mutual comprehension with his alien employers can operate only on a very limited level. Lack of close affinity with the culture of his employer has limited his ability to be responsive to the everyday give and take of communications about the vessel's search.

Consider now a scuba diver. He knows what his submersible equipment can do. He knows how to measure depths, delineate the thermal layers and gradients, measure the speed and directions of the various currents at various levels, and identify and interpret the topography and geology of the ocean floor. He also can identify which fish and other aquatic creatures can be found within particular oceanographic environments. His knowledge helps him to locate the possible presence of predators that can disrupt underwater explorations and operations. Thus, while the scuba diver can never become a fish, he can use a variety of scientific tools to maneuver with purpose within their habitat. His knowledge combined with the use of scientific tools enable identification of which particular fish can be employed in a useful manner. Most importantly, he has a heightened awareness of self and the differentiating factors in his environment that are affecting his search. Because of this heightened awareness, he can more clearly interpret his observations and discoveries to his employers back on the exploration ship.

Some CEOs and other senior corporate executives had difficulty with this approach of hiring a Westerner. They appeared leery and suspicious of Americans who were fluent in the Chinese language and knowledgeable about Chinese culture. It was difficult to understand why they did not see through that prejudice and acknowledge the value of such advantages. Would they frown on U.S. diplomats who possess the language and cultural skills and knowledge that make it possible for them to relate to their foreign counterparts?

Also, when corporate headquarters hired Westerners with such expertise, some mid-level executives, such as product line marketing managers, expressed concerns that this specialist may have "gone native." Fearing their culturally savvy representative may have plunged too deeply into the foreign culture of their targeted Chinese market, they frequently demonstrated behavior indicating that the specialist could not be completely trusted to represent corporate interests. Under these circumstances, the value of his intercultural expertise was considerably diminished.

In my particular case, a well-rounded academic background in Chinese studies was leavened with my undergraduate minor in Marine Transportation, which included exposure to economics, marine insurance, business law, and business management. The latter included a summer's internship working in the home office of a major shipping company. Also, during a vacation break in my seafaring career, I took a job with a marine underwriting firm just to get a taste of that aspect of the maritime industry. And, of course, I had learned a bit about marketing and public relations when working for that Chinese firm in Taiwan. The whole package seemed to provide an interpretative framework that facilitated my way up the learning curve in handling the variety of cross-cultural challenges I faced. Nevertheless, throughout much of my career in China, many business associates viewed me as more of an academic than a businessman. On the other hand, academics regarded me as a commercial person. Actually, I was an adventurer with a good education, and an aptitude for lifelong learning. However, I was now working for an American Fortune 500 company by virtue of my eclectic and somewhat unique background.

Near the beginning of 1981, my boss, the Far Eastern regional director of an American transnational industrial firm, announced that a senior home office executive wanted to visit China. I was instructed to put together a series of fact-finding visits with relevant Chinese business units. Since the senior executive was bringing his wife, my job on this occasion also included arranging tours of cultural sites and shopping excursions. At that time, there were already a considerable number of chairmen, vice chairmen, chief executive officers, chief operating officers, and other senior businessmen beating a path to Beijing. Given this circumstance, I said I needed at least three months lead time for preparations, along with some indication of the company's specific objectives for this trip.

I was given two months and no indication of any particular objectives. Without any guidelines for what this senior guy wanted to achieve, I dug in. This period of China business development for large American transnational companies often involved a popular senior executive mentality. "Gee, if China has such a large market potential and other companies are tapping it, I better go see it. Besides, my wife and I always wanted to visit China." This prevailing attitude, which I called the *See-the-Great-Wall Syndrome,* could be quite useful if you actually needed a senior executive to meet Chinese leaders who wanted to estimate personally the sincerity of corporate intentions, as well as what that company could contribute to China's economic growth. Fortunately, this was the circumstance in which our company's current market development found itself. However, the greatest benefit of this kind of visitation was the opportunity to educate one or more corporate leaders on the problems and peculiarities of the China market, and to lobby for your own ideas on market development.

So, basing our arrangements on the people and units we had been cultivating and doing business with during the previous two years, I moved forward. The plan included a trip to Beijing, Nanjing and Shanghai for our senior executive and his wife. Visits with responsible leaders in various ministries, numerous State-owned industrial enterprises, and foreign trade organizations were set up. Touring arrangements, internal travel, hotels, dinners, banquets, and personal shopping opportunities were organized in great detail. I was designated the trip's official interpreter for our senior executive. I was also told that I would be the minder and the *go-for* at the beck-and-call of his wife—a determined shopper. The plan was set.

To guide our delegation leader, a trip book was put together. This document provided the big boss with a list of the units and people he would be meeting. Also included was a description of each unit's authority and function, and biographical data on the people involved. Talking points that linked our company's multiple industrial capabilities with the specific business and technological interests of the host organizations were suggested. I also provided him with a section on governmental and cultural protocols. Relying on senior executives' commonly held belief that they can be just-in-time experts, I sent the book stateside for his review. The trip book was handed to him when he boarded the airplane heading toward China. At this point, it was up to him to perform.

There was a last minute wrinkle. After the trip book had been sent and while our vice chairman was enroute, one of our ministry-level contacts informed us that our corporate leader would be asked to make a speech. The speech was to be given before a large audience of ministerial, industrial, and foreign trade personnel. This led to something all China hands will have heard of and most will say is apocryphal. Others will claim to have been the perpetrators. All I can say is that I did it in 1981. Volume #2 in my logbook covering my travels throughout the China Mainland from 1980 to 1998, contains a notation to that effect. As the market entry point man, I had to manage the unfolding unexpected wrinkle.

After a brief discussion with our regional director, our big chief from the home office decided that I would interpret his remarks on this occasion rather than relying on the PRC translator whom our hosts would provide. Upon his arrival in Hong Kong, he then asked me if I had any suggestions about what he might say. I opined only that it might not be suitable to follow the Western tradition of starting off a formal presentation with a joke. I pointed out that jokes are culturally imbedded and therefore do not translate well in a different cultural framework. An American joke would make it very difficult for me to carry out my role in transmitting his initial remarks in Mandarin Chinese. Speeches in Chinese culture generally start out quite formally with detailed acknowledgment of those in the audience and of the honor to be addressing them.

Naturally, our vice chairman from the home office commenced his speech with a joke. I think it started with a couple of cowboys rolling into a Texas bar after a difficult trail ride . . .

I did the only thing that could get us quickly past this opening complexity. I said the following, in Mandarin: "Honored guests, my company leader has just told a joke, a common practice when making a speech in American business circles. But, as you know, it would take me at least twenty minutes to elucidate the cultural background that would explain why Americans would find this joke funny. So, if you would be kind enough to help me keep my job, would you all kindly laugh when I finish speaking."

I stopped; they laughed . . . uproariously.

Later, my leader complimented me on translating his joke so well, and with so few words. He actually told me, "I knew you could handle it."

I just smiled and said, "Thank you."

As for the Chinese perspective on this episode, I have learned that Chinese do not expect foreigners to have in-depth knowledge about their culture. They do, however, want to see signs of respect and trustworthiness. It doesn't take all that much effort to show interest in the Chinese way of living. In fact, I would go so far as to say that I concur with contemporary *avant-garde* professional educators who have indicated the rising importance of intercultural competence. Intercultural understanding has become increasingly necessary as our world shrinks with the expansion of modern communications and international trade and investments. Global problem solving entails culturally responsive action on the part of people from all regions of the world. Accordingly, the element of intercultural competency is an essential component of any market entry strategy.

Chapter IV

The Continuity Factor,
or
They Are Always Watching

*—in which I learn how to manage the occasional
manifestation of subcutaneous xenophobia
among the Chinese.*

If belonging to a minority today gives you distinctive status, then I've got everyone beat. How many non-Chinese do you know who can say *sulfamethazine* in Mandarin? If that's not a select group, I don't know what is. In 1982, my company asked me to locate potential suppliers of this intermediate-use chemical in China.

It seemed that my American company's animal health feed additives products utilized some 900 tons of this powdery yellow substance annually. The company's sources were getting too expensive to meet this need. Even worse, our operations team had developed only two production locations worldwide from which to source this product, making the company vulnerable to disruptions in supply. The 600 tons consumed in our American plants came from one of our own factories—in New Jersey— and cost US$13.50 per kilo. A manufacturer in (the then) Yugoslavia, at roughly the same price, produced the 300 tons they utilized in an overseas facility. Corporate strategic planners decided that if a third source could be found, two problems would be resolved. First, costs would be pressured downward. Second, we might be able to reduce or even shut down production of this product in the New Jersey plant. This would be a valuable strategic move because this production line was increasingly expensive to operate under stateside conditions of labor costs and plant upkeep. Furthermore, that production line could be converted easily to other needed, but less costly products.

Identifying sulfamethazine (SM_2) production units in China proved not to be difficult. There was one in Sichuan Province, which claimed to have a couple of hundred tons capacity output. But, it was located well over fifteen hundred kilometers up the Yangtze River. River transport conditions in China at that time were not well suited for international cargo shipping connections. Moreover, with no modern highway system even in the planning stage back then, trucking was out of the question at such distances. Alternative possibilities in China included two plants that claimed to have similar production capacity in Jiangxi and Zhejiang provinces. Preliminary screening indicated that these were suspect in their stated capabilities. This research on SM_2 production units supported the value of having a market entry point man that was not intimately tied to a particular Chinese *guanxi* network. A local agent with familial connections in Zhejiang would do everything possible to ensure we were hooked up with the Zhejiang plant, regardless of that factory's real capacities, or incapacities, with SM2 production. Objective, rigorous analysis would determine the best potential for a production unit that met our needs.

So it transpired that our primary interest was a plant near downtown Beijing—the Beijing No. 2 Pharmaceutical Factory. This plant claimed to have a production capability of 400 tons per year output for SM_2. After screening the unit, another problem arose because my company wanted to import the stuff into the United States. This was problematical because importation of SM_2 required the plant to obtain certified approval from the USFDA. Back in the '80s, to suggest that a Chinese factory apply to an American governmental unit for "approval" of any sort ran up against the virtual Great Wall of Chinese pride and patriotism. During this historical period of modern international business development of the Chinese market, cross-cultural misunderstanding was at work. The Chinese viewed any suggestion of *requiring* foreign government approval processes as an affront. Any such requirement indicated a lack of respect for Chinese sovereignty. Progress on establishing a mutually acceptable deal between this unit and my company would take delicate negotiations.

Preliminary discussions to establish a supplier relationship involved more than the plant leaders of the Beijing No. 2 Pharmaceutical Factory. Discussions also included their Party Secretary and four other decision makers. Two key decision makers were the bosses of their parent unit, the Beijing General Pharmaceutical Corporation, as well as the Pharmaceutical Export Department of the China National Chemicals Import and Export Corporation (referred to in the trade by its telex name, "SINOCHEM"). Naturally, the State Pharmaceutical Administration and the Ministry of Health also got involved with the political facets of this delicate question. Our negotiation strategy involved patient and repetitive explanation of American import requirements, plus the *carrot* of a long-term sales contract with our company. Eventually, this strategy led them to set up an exploratory committee to look into the process and requirements for USFDA approval.

Their committee explorations, in which we participated with much documentation and discussion, ultimately determined that they would undertake three activities. First, their plant would get ready for the USFDA inspection. Second, they would then initiate sampling and testing production runs to our company's product specifications at the No. 2 Factory. And, third, there would have to be lengthy negotiation of export price, quantities, and delivery schedule with SINOCHEM, the official governmental foreign trade body for chemical products.

The first activity involved borrowing our own company's stateside specialist, whose job was to ensure that all our own factories were always up to standard on all regulatory requirements for sanitation and safety. Needless to say, he was delighted to get a couple of free visits to China. His great enthusiasm for working with the No. 2 Factory staff was nurtured with a variety of cultural experiences. Much of our specialist's success was linked to the connections he made with the plant manager and lead technicians while visiting the Great Wall of China, trying out as many Chinese restaurants as we could work into our schedule, and shopping in Beijing's Silk Alley.

The whole process, including preparations for the inspection and price/supply negotiations, ran through the entire year of 1983. When we brought in the USFDA inspector early in January 1984, the Chinese technical team was decidedly focused on achieving success with this inspection. As the USFDA inspector and our entourage walked through a storage room containing a number of monstrously large vats, he commented to me on the visibility of individual vats. Since the catwalks around each vat partially blocked the view of the vat numbers, which were painted *above* the catwalks, he casually mentioned to me that it would probably be better for visibility to have the numbers painted on the vats *below* the catwalks. One of the Chinese staff grabbed my arm and asked, "What'd he say, what'd he say?" I duly translated.

Keeping in mind that the inspector's comment was purely a casual observation, and did not have any bearing on the inspection itself, it came as something of a shock when we passed back through the same storage room about twenty minutes later. Apparently, orders had been issued, and the vat numbers not only had been repainted below the catwalks, but also the numbers previously located *above* the catwalks had been removed. The inspector had the good graces to be a bit embarrassed by their reaction to his offhand comment.

Our friends at the No. 2 Factory passed with flying colors. In fact, the inspector told us that in his entire eight years of inspecting overseas factories, this was the first time he could issue full and unconditional approval on *first* inspection. My company got a three years' supply contract out of the deal. The pricing gave us a cost savings on our total annual SM_2 supply of US$900,000 in the first year's purchase, which amount went straight to our bottom line, with even better savings in subsequent years. As for the No. 2 Factory, they utilized what they learned from us. No. 2 Factory went on to get USFDA approval for a number of other production lines. They became the highest foreign exchange earner of all factories in Beijing Municipality through their exports within a few short years.

But that is not the point of this story. For that, we have to jump ahead some nine years to 1992.

In 1992, I was in my sixth of ten years working in China for the world's largest transnational inspection, testing, and quality assurance company, SGS S.A. (formerly called Société Générale de Surveillance). One of my projects with this company was spearheading the team that negotiated and set up China's first joint venture inspection and testing company. One important developmental objective was to register this new company in the high-tech zone in Beijing so as to benefit from the favorable tax conditions available there. The prize was a corporate tax rate that would be half of the national rate for the life of the company. There would also be a 100 percent tax holiday for the first three years of operation, followed by another three years with a rate one quarter of the standard national rate. The gamble was that we had to register and set up our head office facility in the high-tech zone *before* we could apply for the special tax status.

Our management team was nervous about such a gamble. All our specialized technology was embedded in banks of computers and in the training of our inspection and testing staff. Staff training was the lynchpin for creating the value and excellence of our global quality assurance program. And, quality training of staff rested on the protocols and standards upon which our training programs were built. These training programs, together with confidential and valuable client reports, were archived in our computers. The gamble, then, revolved around the geography of our business and its dependence on computerized and sensitive information. Our inspectors operated primarily in port facilities and manufacturing plants located outside of Beijing. In addition, the laboratories that performed quality testing were not located in Beijing. However, the head office of our joint venture was registered in Beijing. The large bank of computers in this location was designed to record inspection and testing data, and then issue the reports to our clients. How could our sophisticated technical capabilities be demonstrated to the satisfaction of some political types who had no real understanding of the nature of our service business?

When it came time for the *show-and-tell*, there weren't any dramatic visuals as you might find in an electronics production factory for the Chinese officials to observe. Providing documentation for excellence in the service industry is a bit tricky. For example, how could we prove that the sweet, diminutive Beijing girl who served tea during their inspection of our Beijing office facilities had been fully trained in the sampling technologies for inspecting and testing bulk mineral products during the loading of a ship in Tianjin port? Her work had to be done in full accordance with international sampling standards so that our laboratory could verify a uniform product quality in the shipment. Her job was to jump in a van, travel to Tianjin, and go out on the docks where the cargo was being loaded on a ship. This diminutive Beijing girl then had to climb about the loading area with her sampling equipment to get samples for our company lab to test for quality assurance. Fully qualified and well informed, she could do the job down on the docks in Tianjin. But how could her competence be demonstrated inside our Beijing head office? We were decidedly nervous.

Preparing the requisite documentation as best we could, the application was submitted and the Beijing governmental review was duly carried out. They had to send their own inspection team to verify our claim of bringing new and effective technology into the newly established high-tech Beijing Zone. It was then a matter of waiting for a verdict.

About one month later, I was informed that the chief executive of the Beijing high-tech zone, referred to as a district mayor, had invited me to lunch. I had no indication of what to expect. As the market entry point man driving our corporate strategy to prove the service capabilities of Western style quality assurance procedures, I would have to field any number of issues that might be raised. Moreover, our gambit as the first foreign corporation to define a market development need in quality assurance of Chinese products using Western standards in China rested on their understanding that there is a financial value for services *per se*. I steeled myself to handle whatever curveball might be thrown my way and headed to the luncheon appointment on the appointed day.

He had chosen a Peking duck restaurant. Yum. He had nine of his staff with him. Hmmm? I sat down with only one Hong Kong colleague at my side. The Beijing district mayor seemed vaguely familiar, even though I had never been to the high-tech zone district offices. The official application had been the responsibility of our joint venture general manager. He handled all dealings with the high tech zone's office.

After initial introductions and polite formalities, the district mayor cleared his throat, stood up, and in an elaborately formal manner presented me with an official looking envelope. He said that perhaps I didn't remember him, but he remembered me from the year I managed the project to obtain USFDA approval for the SM_2 production line of the Beijing No. 2 Pharmaceutical Factory.

It seems he had been the senior deputy general manager of Beijing General Pharmaceutical Corporation at that time. In that capacity he had the responsibility of overseeing the project to ensure the process had been politically correct according to the Chinese perspective. Given the success of the No. 2 plant, both then and later, he had tracked my career progress during the ensuing years as I traveled around China on a wide variety of developmental projects. I had changed employers, and more than ten years had passed. Nonetheless, when he saw my name on the application documents for this joint venture inspection and testing company, he immediately pre-approved our favorable tax status. We had been given approval even though it was still procedurally necessary to carry out the normal inspection.

We kept in touch. A few years later, he got another promotion, and became one of the several deputy mayors of Beijing Municipality. Our *guanxi* proved to be a very nice relationship for me to have in other circumstances at a later date, but that is another story . . .

While the *serendipity factor* was in play here, there is no doubt that long-term participants in China's foreign business connections are watched, evaluated, and remembered by Chinese officialdom. Those who have a trustworthy reputation can have a positive effect on how their corporate masters are treated by the Chinese powers-that-be. Another example will demonstrate in a surprising fashion how this can work.

Let's return again to the early 1980s. When working for that specialty chemicals company, I was instructed to perform a survey of suture usage in major Chinese hospitals. The product manager back in the home office stateside gave me some rapid training in the technical aspects of silk, catgut, and synthetic polyglycolic acid absorbable sutures. I'm sure you can figure out which one of these was produced by this transnational manufacturing group. After giving me a few guidelines on what questions needed to be asked, I was told to go forth and wangle my way into Chinese surgical operations facilities. I needed to get answers regarding the quantities and types of sutures used in China, and I had to identify where and how they purchased their supplies. And, if I could identify the people who actually handled hospital supplies purchasing, I was to be sure to take them to lunch. Those were my marching orders.

Without going into the gory details, I will mention in passing that Chinese surgeons used silk sutures primarily. (Hey . . . they invented the stuff, didn't they?!) The second choice was catgut, preferably imported from Australia. I was told that Aussie cows, the intestines of which are used to make catgut sutures, graze in meadows that lack the bacteria and bug content of American and European grass, making the Down Under catgut suture stronger and safer to use.

Prior to acquiring this market information, my initial research revealed that it would be necessary for me to obtain permission from various governmental authorities to go into Chinese hospitals. I needed authorization from the Ministry of Public Health, the Chinese Academy of Medical Science, the Ministry of Foreign Economic Relations and Trade, and the State Pharmaceutical Administration. After doing the bureaucratic rounds, my request was passed on to the Party apparatus in each of these institutions. I was told by each unit to wait a few months for an official response. After this circuitous exercise, rather than wait, I walked into the Beijing Hospital, and asked to speak with the chief of surgery.

Dr. Wu Wei-ran was a most amiable person, and he was the hospital director, as well as surgery chief. He listened to what I had to say, and then said, "Let's go for an early dinner together and talk some more." Naturally, we talked a lot about sutures. In the course of our conversation I discovered that, stemming from the surgeon's need for facility with tying knots, his hobby was rope work of all kinds. I could respond knowledgeably to this interest having been a seafarer. I had practical experience with knots, splices, and fancy rope work. The serendipity factor had stuck again! Discussion of our common interest was pleasant and productive. The meal ended with my being invited to attend a couple of surgical procedures on the following day.

Shortly thereafter, Dr. Wu introduced me to his brother, who just happened to be the incumbent president of the Chinese Academy of Medical Science. The door was now open for me. *Guanxi* was at work. Arrangements were made on my behalf, and I was subsequently welcomed into major hospitals in Beijing, Nanjing, Shanghai, and Guangzhou. Market development for polyglycolic absorbable sutures required a unique research opportunity that was amicably afforded to me. In addition to completing my survey months before I received the official approval to conduct it, I made several good friends within the Chinese medical establishment.

I also discovered that many of the surgeons I met were recognized as world-class in their capabilities. Some of these respected surgeons, however, had to work under difficult conditions. For example, after being handed on to the chief surgeon at Rui Jin Hospital in Shanghai, I was invited to scrub in to observe a regularly scheduled surgery. My host told me to feel free to ask questions at any time during the operation. I would be observing the surgical team and how it functioned under the knowledgeable leadership of this skillful surgeon.

It was mid-summer, a very hot and humid time of the year for Shanghai. The surgical theater was in a room on ground level, next to a busy thoroughfare. I scrubbed in as was required of everyone in the theater. I also observed that stringent sterilization procedures on all surgical tools were in place. However, the windows to the outside were open, and clouds of motor exhaust were drifting into the room. When I asked Professor Dong why the windows were open, he looked up at me, smiled sadly and gently, and explained, "The staff requires it because we have no air conditioning."

What you need to understand here is that during the Great Proletarian Cultural Revolution (1966–1976), this trained professional had been sent to a remote rural area for "re-education." Having been deemed an "intellectual"—apparently a great political crime, he was kept there for ten years. This was the time when the youthful mobs of undisciplined radicals had been turned loose on the country by Chairman Mao Zedong for the purpose of rooting out political reactionaries. Professor Dong was required to perform medical procedures with less than adequate facilities for half of each day under the direction of ignorant teenagers. These callous youths decided who would receive medical attention based primarily on the political correctness of the people seeking medical assistance. The other half-day was spent in menial duties prescribed by his mostly illiterate jailers. He specifically mentioned slopping hogs, mucking out stables, shoveling human waste, and undertaking kitchen duties as part of his political re-education. He said he had not been unaffected by this experience.

Throughout this period, I met with Dr. Wu in Beijing several times. We enjoyed each other's company, and shared discussions on the arts, traditions, and histories of our respective cultures. On one occasion, I gave him a gift appropriate to our common interest in the nautical arts. It was a second edition of the *Encyclopedia of Knots and Fancy Rope Work* (1942) that I had in my personal library. He was quite pleased. And I was pleased to share in thought-provoking intercultural discussions that enriched my understanding of Chinese and Western worldviews.

We kept in touch over the ensuing years, even after I left the chemical specialties company to join the inspection company. During our occasional private lunches, which sometimes included his wife, he would ask penetrating questions. These questions included inquiries about the nature of the business in which I was involved and the nature of the problems I was experiencing with the development of our business in China. On one occasion, I told him that a senior home office executive was planning a visit to China. I had been asked to arrange for him to have a luncheon with a particular vice premier on the State Council, but so far my approaches had not been successful.

After I told Dr. Wu of my dilemma, he confided that ever since his official retirement, his job was to guard the health of China's elder statesmen. In fact, those whose physical condition warranted close monitoring needed his approval before they were cleared to engage in potentially tiring or stressful travel or meetings. Dr. Wu thought a moment, and then said, "Give me a choice of dates and I'll see what can be done. Also, you'll need to invite me when you organize the luncheon." The vice premier attended, and the meeting went off quite nicely for all concerned.

Guanxi is definitely a lifetime commitment.

Chapter V

The Middleman Mentality,
or
The Occasional Stinker Is Not Necessarily
on the Other Side of the Table

—in which we learn whom
not to trust.

Amiddleman can be identified by several names. The middleman may be broker, agent, or advisor. He is anyone from outside the company who sets up arrangements for any sort of transaction on behalf of the company. Those who serve in this role in the West understand that they are a highly disposable commodity. In fact, middlemen are intensely aware that when two principals get together, the first thing they are most likely to agree upon is to dump the middleman.

Many consultants morph into middlemen during a project. This can be beneficial if they have contacts that can help you achieve your business objectives. However, it is vital that you have sufficient oversight to ensure they stick to the agenda you are paying them to facilitate. Quite frankly, they can very easily highjack your efforts into a direction more suitable to their own goals if you are not monitoring their activities. This is a matter of "controlling the controllables," an important principle in any endeavor.

In China, the middleman has a more secure role due to a fundamental cultural trait. Specifically, social harmony, no matter how superficial a phenomenon it may be in reality, is valued over open conflict. Thus, it is the middleman's primary function to deflect confrontation, absorb emotional eruptions, coax negotiators away from non-negotiable positions, and thus preserve the veneer of harmony between and among principal cooperators. The innate traditional Chinese social *modus operandi* of *guanxi* helps to protect the middleman's vital role during business development.

The choice of who should serve as middleman can be either accidental or deliberate, depending on the situation. Both methods have their hazards. An experience that occurred during one of my first trips as an assistant to the East Asian regional general manager of the previously mentioned chemicals firm may help to elucidate this axiom. In the early 1980s we were searching the China market for opportunities to introduce our company's elastomers and other such chemical additives for rubber products. My boss, a Welshman with a flamboyantly gregarious approach to life, had not yet learned to trust my linguistic capabilities. He had hired a local Chinese agent to handle interpreting during the business meetings we had scheduled.

Our first meeting was at a truck tire manufacturing facility in Shanghai. While hard to believe, my boss's introductory comments, and our agent's translation of those comments, went something like this:

> **Boss** (*speaking in English*): "As the regional head of my company, I wanted to meet you personally to learn about your product development needs, and to introduce you to some of our unique rubber product additives that can improve the safety and longevity of your truck tires."

> **Agent** (*supposedly translating into Chinese*): "I am the agent for the American company that this gentleman heads up in the Far East. I am also the agent for a German company, which has many products that can help improve your manufacturing capabilities and save you money."

> **Boss:** "We would not only be happy to meet with your Research & Development team, but also we can send you product samples and a technical team that can run pilot tests in your own laboratory to demonstrate the

performance capabilities of our additives."

Agent (*again, supposedly translating into Chinese*): "I have with me the complete catalogue from my German principal, which I can leave with you and come back later to discuss."

It went on this way until our first break, at which time I gave my boss a brief review of what our interpreter was saying. Needless to say, I was taken off the bench and sent in as a relief pitcher for the rest of the game. This was the first of several business encounters that enlightened my boss on the cautionary tale of determining trustworthy middlemen. These encounters also made a strong case for having a scuba diver as a member of the in-house market-entry crew. It certainly helps to have someone onboard who can understand the deeper parts of the water in which you are trolling.

Another example:

In the second half of the 1990s, much later in my China business development career, it was my job to help find a China market entry strategy for a major American insurance company. At that time, China was handing out only two insurance business licenses each year to foreign companies. My company was something like number eighty-nine on the applications queue, which was maintained by PRC governmental officials that issued the licenses. Do the math. This was not an acceptable position.

During the period of research to develop ideas for a viable strategic plan to "jump the queue," one of our top executives in the home office back in the States decided he knew a perfect middleman to move us forward. This senior home office executive instructed us to meet with the China-based representative of the company's primary stateside bank. We were told that our company's close connection with this bank made their agent a reliable and trustworthy resource. It seems that he had a "great investment opportunity" that would get us into China business "without the need to obtain a China business license." Or, at least, that was what we were told by that home office "authority."

Together with a colleague who was an insurance specialist, we met the gentleman in his Hong Kong office. This Cantonese gentleman, who had received his advanced education in the United States, did have a unique offer to make. He described a new consortium, formed in Beijing, consisting of nineteen Chinese manufacturers of a variety of products. The consortium's purpose was to set up a self-insurance group. Eighteen of the participants had committed to putting five percent each into the initial capital investment pot. The nineteenth investor was to put in the final ten percent. The strategy for getting us into the Chinese insurance market was tied to this ten percent Chinese investor.

Apparently, there was some sort of connection between this nineteenth investor and the representative for the stateside bank of our head office. This ten percent investor was looking to find a foreign financial body to take up five percent of the venture. The proposed deal was that the nineteenth investor would be the nominal, *i.e.*, legal, owner for both his remaining five percent and the foreign firm's five percent investment. As the legal owner, the named ten percent investor would control the board seat. This was the device that would supposedly put the foreign firm "into" China. We were assured that there would be no need for our company name to appear on the capital investment documentation. The named nineteenth investor would be providing us with a great market entry opportunity by controlling the ten percent and managing decisions on our behalf.

Yeah, right . . .

This bank official also had a document in front of him, which he said was a signed authorization from this nineteenth investor for him to negotiate the terms of our investment. This document supposedly also outlined the key terms of the business arrangement that would be acceptable to both parties. He seemed to be implying, "Trust me; no need for those tedious negotiations."

Even though I was able to discern that his authorization document was bogus, we overtly had to treat this proposal with respect because of the close business connection between the bank rep's company and our headquarters back in America. We therefore thanked him for his time and his offer. Explaining that we would have to report on his proposal to our senior executives back in the States, we went to lunch, and *then* cracked up with laughter.

This situation is an excellent example of the dangers facing a foreign corporation in a culturally different environment. It was patently obvious that this bank representative, a Chinese national, fully expected us to take his proposal as a good deal. From his cultural perspective of *guanxi*, he apparently expected his connection to, and influence within, our home office would enable him to complete this duplicitous deal. In this case, it appeared that he held contempt for the intelligence of Westerners working the China trade. His attitude was barely concealed. As a shirtsleeve sinologist swapping stories with other China hands, I have come to believe that similar cases can result as much from cultural ignorance as from outright attempts to snooker the culturally divergent businessman.

So, why were we laughing?

That potential middleman with *guanxi* into our company through his employer—the stateside bank—was more of a double agent than a middleman. He had manipulated the relationship between his employer and our employer—the stateside insurance company. He was selling the fiction that he had found a way for us to achieve our company's goal of investing in a China insurance operation. It was a ploy to establish the illusion that he was acting in our company's best interests. In actuality, he was trying to sell us an illegal and very bad deal on behalf of his Beijing connections.

This "investment opportunity" was a kind of self-insurance scheme for businesses that were uninsurable with regular insurance providers. Some of the participants produced munitions, which were exported to countries hostile to the United States. Some were coal-mining operations, which were notorious for their unsafe working conditions.

Whereas this example happened to be perpetrated by a Chinese, please do not assume this kind of duplicity is tied to one culture. It occurs everywhere all the time. While working in Asia, I had numerous experiences with dubious business opportunities proposed by a variety of businessmen from a variety of cultures, including American. The world of commerce and profit making invites people of all kinds from all parts of the world. With China's amazing economic growth averaging a 10 percent or more increase each year throughout this period, businessmen from around the globe scurried in and out of commercial metropolises like Hong Kong, Shanghai, Nanjing, Guangzhou, and Beijing. There is no doubt that opening the China market to outsiders raised the "Let's-make-a-deal" mentality to an intense level.

Perhaps one other point about middleman relationships in China should be mentioned here. There is an increasing number of foreigners, both Americans and Europeans, who have spent the time and effort to become knowledgeable about Chinese language and culture, and who are serving in roles that facilitate positive cross-cultural communication. Some Western businessmen are quick to perceive the value of this kind of specialized assistance and leadership. The Chinese themselves also acknowledge the sincerity of people committed to a long-term effort to facilitate mutually beneficial cross-cultural cooperation. At the same time, some Asian individuals who make their living in the middleman role seem threatened by Westerners who have more than a superficial understanding of China. Some of them will react by dismissing the foreign point man with near overt contempt. Others, like our banker friend described above, will try to exploit what they see as naïveté to gain an advantage.

In some situations, internal organizational obstructions can inadvertently get into the middle of your business development efforts. This often occurs in ways that can prove most unfortunate for your company. Sometimes, too, it is not inadvertent action but rather personal political posturing among executives that rankles and subsequently impedes business development. The example in this case goes back to my earliest days working the China mainland.

It should be stated up front that my seven years' tenure with the American specialty chemicals company gave me the opportunity to earn my spurs in China business development. I am grateful for that experience to the president of the international division who hired me "on spec" so to speak. Curiously, part of my career turned out to be cleaning up messes made by senior executives who wanted to score a *big China deal* on their own. This helped me develop skills in spotting the proverbial red flags and mine-fields in the China business environment. As a highly diversified Fortune 500 company, my employer had many divisions competing for market growth and record sales. The many division heads and regional market managers saw China as a ripe market that they could develop.

This particular company's matrix-management organization built inevitable confusion into our command structure. There was a great deal to learn internally when problem solving. In matrix-management, strategic and tactical decisions were often being made by conflicting egos, and not by a clear hierarchy with a respect for careful research and analysis. In fact, what I observed there was often a distressing lack of due diligence among many senior executives when it came to doing business in China. Moreover, management initiatives were not always coordinated in the head office despite their intent to do so.

Management of the exploration of the China market, in terms of learning which of the company's products would be suitable for local needs, had been given over to the general manager of their Far East division, based in Hong Kong. Since I reported to him, I was also based in Hong Kong. Most of the time, however, I thrashed about China with a briefcase filled with product specifications from various product divisions. These included industrial chemicals, agricultural chemicals, animal feed additives, pharmaceuticals, and surgical specialties. My internal working partners were product managers and technical sales representatives from our various product line divisions.

There were, however, some product divisions that were independent of the company's system of international subsidiaries. One such division manufactured synthetic fibers for the textiles industry. Its president managed to make a connection with the (then) sole Chinese agency that handled all raw materials sourcing for China's weaving mills. His connection was based in the New York office of the China National Textiles Import and Export Corporation. Those in the China trade referred to this unit as "CHINATEX"—a name derived from their telex address. This division president was confident in his connections and his ability to drive sales for his division.

Without any courtesy communication with my boss, the Far East regional head, this division president single-handedly concluded a sales contract with the CHINATEX representative based in New York. The contract amounted to several million dollars worth of synthetic fibers. This appeared to be a smashing coup for him personally. Regrettably, there is more to concluding a sales contract than simply agreeing to terms on paper and then signing off on them. The product described in the contract must actually reach the buyer, so appropriate follow-up steps must be in place to see that delivery occurs. These steps, of course, affect the margin of profit; and this division president was looking to make record sales.

Unfortunately, a mistake was made when the contracted product specifications were transmitted to the company's plant in Spain that manufactured these fibers. Apparently, steps were not in place to reconfirm accurate specifications. The fibers were supposed to be cut to a specified length, with a given variation tolerance. For whatever reason, the plant got it wrong. Moreover, no steps were in place for pre-shipment inspection. The plant shipped product that didn't conform to the fiber length specifications in the purchase contract. No one had made any kind of pre-shipment inspection to ensure that the product met the contract's technical requirements.

We first learned about the situation *after* the head-man in CHINATEX's import department, located in Beijing, blasted our company. The error had been discovered only after the shipment landed in Tianjin port, and our company had already cashed CHINATEX's Letter of Credit. The understandably irritated general manager in Beijing telexed his complaint to our fibers division president, and threatened to blackball the entire company from doing any business in China. Given China's political structure, there was no doubt he could make that happen. This was no idle threat. At that point, someone in our stateside home office thought to let our Hong Kong office know that "we" had a serious problem.

It was not sufficient that the home office sent a return telex offering to send another shipment with the correct specifications. The CHINATEX boss man wanted a personal apology in Beijing. Our Far East general manager was instructed to solve the problem since it was *his* territory. So, *I* was told to serve as his delegate to fix the problem, and sent to Beijing. The situation reminded me of some old military wisdom, which noted what "flows downhill."

At this point, I must remind you of the traditional Chinese attitude toward age: older folks expect respect. Add to that the probable attitude of a PRC government executive, who is most likely to be very sensitive to any signs, apparent or real, of foreign disrespect. Then, picture a foreigner in his forties seeking an interview with a Chinese senior official who was more than seventy years old. Add the stressful objective of solving a multi-million dollar problem and preventing a transnational firm's entire China market entry program from being axed. My gut told me we should not add insult to injury. As my company's emissary, I had to figure out how to communicate our apology sincerely and forge a new alliance that assured a positive working relationship for ongoing market development.

Fortunately, I knew that rather than presenting myself as an authorized representative with the authority to negotiate a formal resolution of the problem, I would act in the manner of a middle-man *a la Chinoise*. I would be the messenger whose function was merely to understand the full nature and depth of the problem. It would not be my place to defend my company or make apologies. My ostensive purpose in asking for the meeting was to ensure my principal understood the problem correctly. The Chinese senior manager could vent his anger without fear of losing face; without putting himself into a position from which he could not withdraw. It would not be a confrontational situation between our two companies.

Somehow I also had the good fortune of knowing someone who could help me contact the right CHINATEX staff who could influence their boss to give me the courtesy of an interview. A little *guanxi* goes a long way.

The meeting started with me being the recipient of a one-hour-and-five-minutes-long lecture by this senior PRC official. He lectured with considerable passion. He recited the history of imperialist aggression, the violations of Chinese sovereignty committed by the imperialist powers, the determination of the Chinese government to prevent any future such evils on their soil, the arrogance of capitalist agents, and our disrespect for the needs of the Chinese people on whose behalf he worked. I listened intently and respectfully. I made no excuses. Nothing interrupted the strong flow of his words and thoughts.

I didn't argue. Chinese Communist Party members have had lots of experience in both giving and receiving long harangues of an ideological nature. It also was obvious that he had been pre-briefed on the full range of business activities in which our company was engaged in China. He knew where we had gone, and what our various business interests were. We had been correct in our understanding of his ability to close the entire China market to our company. I maintained a respectful attitude, listened attentively, and conversed directly in Chinese, without the need of the interpreter that they had provided. With the promise of a correct replacement shipment as speedily as possible, our meeting concluded with his stating that he would accept a reshipment without further difficulties for my company. In effect, I had acted as an *ad hoc* middleman *a la Chinoise* by absorbing and deflecting confrontational contact between the two concerned principal individuals. That apparently was enough to fix our dilemma.

CHINATEX got a reshipment of synthetic fibers. My company did not get blackballed in China. The division president who put us into this mess got a bonus and a promotion. I got to keep my job.

And, I learned that acting as an *ad hoc* middleman *a la Chinoise* can be an effective tool.

All three of these examples of how a middleman can affect situations have another common element. In each story, a senior executive created the situation in which a middleman became involved.

I've often been asked to describe the most difficult aspect of China business development work. I would have to say that during the early decades of China's opening to the West, the single most difficult recurring problem was dealing with the Euro-American cultural perspective, primarily among the corporate leaders. I think the average "China Hand" doing jobs similar to mine would express it differently. They would probably say something like, "My biggest headache is the twits back in the home office! They just don't understand that you have to approach things differently out here!" Generally speaking, the Western bottom-line mentality seems to require speed when making deals. In the East, however, cultivating a comfortable relationship comes first. The front-line troops must have perseverance, and their bosses back home need to learn patience.

Home office hiccups can be as simple as not considering time zone differences. I recall the time when my boss groused to me of receiving a phone call at 3:00 AM from a senior executive back in New Jersey. When Ernie complained about the time, the caller apologized and explained, "Aw, Ernie, gimme a break. I can never remember if you're twelve hours ahead or twelve hours behind."

While educating people about time differences can be relatively easily, other home office gaffs can result from organizational situations beyond anyone's control. For example, the home office of the chemical and pharmaceuticals company I worked for in the early eighties advised us that they would be interested in setting up a joint-venture manufacturing plant for surgical supplies in China. The suture usage survey I carried out was one of the preliminaries that led to this proposed project. The primary product for such a facility would be a synthetic absorbable surgical suture. This stuff was made with polyglycolic acid, and was used for subcutaneous wound closures. Once put in, the body would gradually absorb it—no suture removal needed.

We approached the organization in Beijing that ran the Beijing No. 2 Pharmaceutical Factory, i.e., the Beijing General Pharmaceutical Corporation. You'll recall that we had already shared a very positive experience with them on purchasing their sulfamethazine. As we expected, they were very interested in our proposal, and we started the preliminaries for a feasibility study. Both sides were on a steep learning curve because Sino-foreign joint ventures were a new idea in China at that time in history. It would take a great deal of time to get it right. Nevertheless, we were approaching the project with lots of patience and good will on both sides.

The home office back in New Jersey was having difficulty understanding why our progress was slow. They had no experience with even the basic logistics inside China. Back then, just to send one telex from Beijing to the States could take you anywhere from three to four hours thanks to the procedure dictated by the government. The procedure was ungodly. It involved going to the one and only available post office that contained public telex facilities, and going through a series of three or four very long queues, each with a differing function in the official process, just to send out one message.

A top home office executive got impatient and decided to send one of their senior engineers out to China to help speed up the process because he was Chinese and spoke Chinese. This seemed both reasonable and appropriate to him. However, we, the guys in the field, were not advised about this decision. Furthermore, that top executive did not consider the implications of this engineer having been raised in Taiwan. The engineer's family was originally from Jiangsu Province—Suzhou, I think. His parents had come to Taiwan in 1950 around the time when the Chinese Nationalists were driven out of the Mainland by the People's Liberation Army. So, that's where he headed—Jiangsu, where he could warm up some of his own *guanxi* network. He had extended family there.

Before anyone knew it, he had signed a Letter of Intent on behalf of the company for establishing a joint venture with a local factory in Jiangsu. That stopped our progress in Beijing. The mere appearance of duplicity on the part of our home office management stimulated the distrust that killed Beijing's interest. Nothing was said or done overtly. The people with whom we were working just became unavailable due to "other priorities."

The Taiwanese engineer's project in Jiangsu went nowhere. He had avoided any cooperation or coordination with the Far East regional manager and his team. Also, his own division back in the home office offered no backup or support to sustain the effort.

In fact, that particular division had no business responsibilities related to the China market. The authorization for his exploratory trip had come from somewhere up in the rarified air of the corporate boardroom. As far as I was concerned, this unfortunate mess was the direct result of an unhealthy union of authority and ignorance.

It was shortly after that I decided to accept a job offer from the inspection and testing company, SGS, to head up their China Division. The chemical company's rudderless China initiatives eventually drifted off course.

A couple of years prior to this change, an old friend on the China circuit, Fred Schneiter, came up with another application of the middleman function. His idea was to use a China point man from a different company to help him educate his own home office boss. He said the idea was based on that old proverb, "A prophet is never honored in his own country." Apparently, Fred did not think some of his messages to headquarters were fully understood. As the East Asian head of U.S. Wheat Associates, a not-for-profit advocate for promoting American wheat exports, he also traveled widely around China.

We did a lot of note comparing on our respective China adventures, usually with much mirth. On one occasion, he got serious—a rare occurrence with Fred. He told me a delegation of his boss and a group of wheat exporters was coming in from the States, and he was setting up their China tour. He wanted to organize a reception for them in Hong Kong before they all headed off to Beijing. His objective was to use that occasion to introduce his boss to a couple of key ideas about how best to communicate with the Chinese leadership. Apparently, Fred felt that his boss functioned with assumptions about China that were residue from Cold War days.

Fred's idea was simple. I would get an invitation to the reception. His boss would get the opportunity to extract information from an active "China hand" that was being paid by someone else. In effect, I would be Fred's middleman between him and his boss. He mentioned certain areas where his boss had some wrong-headed notions, and then left it to me to guide our friendly chat over cocktails. The idea was to have somebody else's "prophet" answer questions and chat about what works and what does not work in China.

Later, Fred told me that he was quite satisfied with the results of his little stratagem. He reflected, "It didn't resolve all my concerns, but it did make him a bit more receptive to learning about how things are done out here." I paused a moment, and then said, "Say, Fred, next month I've got a couple of senior guys from our home office coming in for a visit. Would you be available to attend a reception? I could use a little help, too."

The company I served at that time had widely diverse product and project interests, which necessitated a multitude of exploratory probes into this unknown potential market. Unfortunately, these various efforts never coalesced into a coherent management vision that would coordinate operations within a network of continuously cultivated personal connections among relevant Chinese organizations. Strong interest and support by corporate leadership was needed to create that vision and ensure effective internal communications across product line divisions. This did not happen during my tenure in their service.

I liken this first experience on the China mainland to my first trip to sea as a cadet-midshipman on a steam-powered freighter on the India run back in 1959. That ship was a maintenance nightmare—a real rust bucket. But, because the work involved continuous nursing of almost all the gear and equipment on board, I got to learn a great deal about the inner workings of vessel management. Likewise, as a junior management-level employee in that multinational chemical company, my observations of what worked, and what did not work, in their attempts at China market entry informed my growth as a China business development specialist.

Chapter VI

Chinese Hospitality, or Grin and Bear It

—in which I get very wet on the upper reaches of the Yellow River.

Chinese hospitality can be a bit overwhelming. Empathic souls see this phenomenon as stemming from a profound desire on the part of the Chinese to ensure that their guests, especially those coming from other countries, are looked after well. There's also the effort to make a good impression. This view is given ancient sanction by that oft-quoted line from the *Analects of Confucius*: "Is it not delightful to have friends come from afar?"

The more cynical types are a bit suspicious of all the fanfare. The cynical viewpoint considers Chinese hospitality as a means of establishing a psychological dominance, which in turn creates a distraction from the focus of establishing a good business deal.

However, positive, mutually respectful relationships form the basis of all interaction from the Chinese perspective. Chinese hospitality is intended to facilitate the development of such relationships. In addition to familiarizing Western visitors with historical and cultural sites, the special cuisine of the local region offers a point of pride for Chinese hosts. Regional cuisine is shared with elaborate presentation on a large round table with an over-sized rotating lazy susan to ensure everyone partakes of each of the many Chinese dishes.

Having traveled to some sixty-two Chinese cities during my business career, I have had my full share of the courtesy and warmth of numerous government officials and other professionals. In fact, on the occasion of one particular whirlwind marketing trip, I experienced seven Chinese banquets (of no less than ten courses each) in five towns over a twelve-day period. Chinese hospitality frequently fetes the foreign visitor with gastronomical feasts of gigantic proportions. Often these feasts are supported with unique cultural experiences as well.

Over the years, my visits have been showered with local delicacies such as deep fried scorpions in Tianjin, bear paw and moose nose in Harbin, a sort of muddled earthworm dish in Xining, and a stew in Guangzhou, the contents about which I refused to inquire. Sometimes there are occasions in which ignorance is most probably a blessing.

I did, however, notice that there was one delicacy, of great favor throughout China, which was served at almost every banquet—everywhere I went. In Chinese, it is called *hai-sheng*. The French call it *beche-de-mer*. Malays and Aussies know it as *trepang*. The dictionaries euphemistically explain it as "sea cucumber." In reality, it's a sea slug.

The Chinese like their sea slugs boiled, dried, or smoked—in soup or in sauce. They know full well that most foreigners, even those with ubiquitous tastes, find them aesthetically questionable. But they are expensive by Chinese standards. And, in most cases, a government official can justify their inclusion on the menu only when they are entertaining special guests. As a result, the foreigner will be given first dibs on sampling this delicacy, after which his hosts will scoop up the remainder with great gusto.

The key to banquet survival is to remember that if you clean up a serving of a particular dish, you will most certainly get an immediate refill with the same stuff. Thus, volume control is achieved by leaving a bit of each dish untouched on your plate. Ensuring no one goes away hungry is a Chinese cultural imperative. Put another way, if you had a Jewish mother, a Chinese banquet could make you a bit homesick.

The other minefield is drink. Once you accept an alcoholic beverage, you are fair game for repeated toasts. This problem has been alleviated somewhat in more recent years, since the government has encouraged a more moderate approach to banqueting. Nevertheless, it pays to exercise a degree of caution with the more celebratory aspects of your business socializing.

After that meeting at the truck-tire plant in Shanghai described above, my boss and I went on to a similar facility in Nanjing. Our hosts threw a welcome banquet. There were two of us and five of them at the standard circular festive board. As the meal progressed, each of the Chinese stood up and toasted my boss, one after another. And, it was *gan bei,* literally "dry glass," every time. He, being a good sport, responded positively—not noticing that after each one of them had one drink apiece, he had consumed five. I might also note that they were drinking *maotai.*

I got the job of steering my boss back to his hotel room. The following morning, after the pain subsided, he came up with a variation on the concept of the "designated driver." He determined that he would have a "designated drinker." I was awarded that job for all our subsequent business meals in China. My survival in this role sometimes involved a pre-banquet meeting with the guy in charge of the kitchen. I would make a private deal so that the *maotai* bottle used to refill my glass was actually filled with water only. I learned this trick from my counterpart at the Chinese Ministry of Agriculture during my first business trip to Beijing back in 1980. This subterfuge was necessary because all bilingual participants at a Chinese banquet are expected to serve as unofficial communications facilitators for the people at their respective tables. A clear head is required to fulfill this role.

There is a traditional defense against *gan bei.* One can respond by saying *sui yi,* which means, "as much as you like." At that point, you are free to just take a sip without causing any loss of

face to anyone. However, this retort is more generally appropriate for women, elderly men, or people considered to have frail
health. I used it without shame when in the company of Chinese
miners. Those guys are really tough drinkers. Whereas your Chinese friends will be suitably impressed by your knowledge of an
historically sanctioned cultural *riposte,* you must take care not to
overuse it. By accepting a full *gan bei,* you communicate strength
and encouragement for all those present to enjoy themselves fully.

A classic case study on Chinese hospitality happened years later,
after I joined that inspection, testing, and quality assurance services
firm. Their clients worldwide had been pressing them to extend
their services into China. Unfortunately, the Chinese Inspection
Law at that time stated unequivocally, "No foreign inspection
company shall be established within the People's Republic of
China." I was hired in 1986 to spearhead the development and
execution of a market entry strategy that would circumvent that
obstruction—a virtual Great Wall.

The Inspection Law was the legal basis for a PRC government
monopoly on cargo inspections. The agency that carried out these
government-required inspections was called the China National
Import and Export Commodities Inspection Bureau—normally
referred to as "CCIB." Government-required inspections were
ostensibly for the purpose of protecting the health and welfare of
the Chinese people and China's economy. Our difficulty was that
private inspection companies are hired by commercial entities to
perform inspections for commercial reasons. Thus, they served to
protect the interests of the buyers and/or sellers of specific goods
in specific transactions. We needed to be able to get our inspectors
into Chinese ports to carry out third-party commercial verifica-
tions of the quantity and quality of our clients' shipments.

It is very difficult to explain, much less sell, the idea of the
place and value of an independent, third-party, commercial
inspection in a society where what Westerners would regard as

a conflict-of-interest is seen as culturally reasonable, as well as a competitive advantage. A CCIB inspector was under no obligation to inform a foreign buyer of any deficiencies in exported Chinese products, and usually did not. This precept was the heart of our company's challenge and my focus as the corporate cross-cultural trouble-shooter.

CCIB leadership steadfastly refused to admit that our work did not compete with their governmental function. However, when they learned that the fees for our commercial inspections were paid in hard US dollars or Swiss francs, they pulled a commercial unit out of their hat. Called the China National Import and Export Commodities Inspection *Corporation* (CCIC), the actual inspectors in this agency were in fact government employees of CCIB. This was not a problem for us. In fact, my company immediately jumped on the opportunity to negotiate a cooperative agreement with this "commercial" unit. This agreement called for us to sub-contract inspection assignments to them. The subcontract included the proviso that our inspectors would be permitted to accompany their inspectors as "observers" and "technical consultants." This form of operational cooperation was euphemistically called a "technical exchange"—a perfectly legal activity. In actuality, our inspectors did the work and wrote up the reports that went to our clients. Naturally, we had to share the fees with CCIC, but we now had one foot in the door.

The actual *modus operandi* was for our "technical consultant" to perform the inspection, and issue the inspection report to the client on our own letterhead, with a copy to CCIC. The latter would then copy our report on their letterhead and solemnly hand it over to us, along with an invoice for their share of the inspection fee. The CCIC report was respectfully filed away for future reference.

A major part of my function became the maintenance of a positive working relationship with CCIC. I also had to work at deflecting their observations of other, more strategic, movements designed to promote better market access for my employers. Students of military history and strategic thought will understand the importance of pinning the center while preparing a flanking maneuver. The objective of that flanking maneuver would be to break the Chinese monopoly.

Meanwhile, we added to our technical exchange work. We decided to cooperate with CCIC on promotional activities. This cooperation was an essential ingredient for our eventual success in China. Chinese importers, exporters, and foreign trade administrators had no knowledge of the value and purpose of commercial inspections. To them, an import or export inspection was a government requirement for which they had to pay a fee to the government agency, CCIB. They needed to be educated. To that end, we proposed to CCIC that we create a one-day seminar on this subject and take it to as many industrial centers and ports as our respective promotional budgets would allow. The result was a *dog-and-pony show* that was designed and implemented by us with their endorsement. Entitled *How to Avoid Risks in International Trade,* our presentations appeared in twenty-eight cities over an eighteen-month period, commencing in 1988.

The message was a simple one. Suppose a Chinese importer wanted to buy, say, a shipload of fishmeal from Chile for use in aquaculture. Normally, the seller would require the buyer to open a Letter of Credit at a bank to guarantee that the funds would be transmitted to the seller as soon as the terms of sale were fulfilled. The buyer's guarantee would be to require that a third-party inspection service check the product, usually ex-factory or at port of loading, to ensure that the quantity and quality matched what was stipulated in the Purchase Contract. The bank would be required not to release the funds until they received the original Certificate of Inspection and other relevant shipping documentation. Our program was designed to teach this idea using actual case studies from international trade.

The two lead speakers in our program were a CCIC vice president and myself, the representative of the cooperating foreign inspection company. When we started the series, the CCIC representative would first explain the purpose and function of his parent organization, CCIB. My marketing manager, a Hong Kong Chinese, and I would then relate well-researched and documented cases of fraud and disaster. Each case either could have been, or actually was, prevented by careful application of third-party commercial inspection. Since I, an American, spoke directly in Chinese, I became a featured attraction, even an occasional minor luminary, on local TV stations. Nevertheless, we made the program truly educational.

However, as our traveling circus matured, the CCIC vice president, who was the first speaker in our program, would steal the case studies we explained in our previous performances. Using them as if they were his own research, he started to sell CCIC as a true commercial inspection agency. My colleague and I politely ignored this blatant plagiarism and continued to gather new and different stories from our worldwide network of subsidiaries to use at each *next* stop in our travels. After each performance, one of us would get on the phone to our Hong Kong office where an assistant had been busily contacting our various other offices around the world, gathering more case studies for us to use. That assistant, Ms. Bonnic Leung, was worth her weight in gold. She enabled us to keep our part of the show fresh and new with each performance, while avoiding any confrontation with our plagiarizing traveling companion.

This sensitivity to the Chinese valuation of non-confrontational relationships, combined with my having taught our CCIC traveling companions how to play the card game called *Hearts* on the long train rides between cities, helped to develop a camaraderie among our combined team. This camaraderie proved to be quite valuable later when we were faced with more serious and significant problems in our "cooperative" endeavors.

Early on in these marketing efforts, we arrived at Lanzhou, the capital of Gansu Province. At that time, Lanzhou was small by Chinese standards, with a population of a little over two million. The boundary of Gansu forms a long, thin province in the north-central highlands, with grasslands and mountains. It connects a high plateau and the upper reaches of the Yellow River with the deserts of Xinjiang. For centuries Gansu has been the beginning of China's communications corridor with central and western Asia. The ancient Silk Road started there. Its main industries, based primarily on metals and minerals processing, were prime candidates for third-party inspection as their bulk cargo export business and corresponding machinery import requirements grew.

The local CCIB branch and provincial Foreign Trade Bureau shared the hosting duties. They picked us up at the airport, got us settled in an old moldy guesthouse of Soviet-period vintage, and took us immediately to the welcome banquet. As we got to know each other between the many toasts to friendship and cooperation and chatted about our respective personal experiences in life, it came out that my seafaring experience earlier in life had given me great interest in and pleasure from boating activities. They immediately stated they would be delighted to arrange for a short excursion on the Yellow River right after the conclusion of our program, and before our departure to our next destination. I was very pleased with this particular display of Chinese hospitality.

The next afternoon, following the conclusion of our educational endeavors, we were put into a minivan and started off to our special treat. Keep in mind that my Hong Kong colleague and I were both still dressed in three-piece suits with our briefcases in hand. Our suitcases had already been packed and stowed on the minivan for our imminent exit from Lanzhou by rail. Our next gig was in Xi'an—the home of the ancient Terracotta Warriors exhibition.

The vehicle stopped at a somewhat desolate stretch of mud flats north of town. Without explanation, we were escorted out over the long shallow slope of mud leading down to the river's edge. Somewhat puzzled, we saw no pier or quay in either direction along that stretch of the river. Instead, drawn up on the shoreline, was a small, open-decked raft with a surface area not much bigger than the foyer in a Nebraska prairie house. The mismatched, rough-hewn planks of the deck were laid over and tied to six hand-sewn and tar sealed goatskin bags that had been blown up with air to make the craft float. I had seen a sketch of that vessel design in a book during a course on naval architecture at the United States Merchant Marine Academy many years ago. Our excursion boat was a replica of a Neolithic period raft.

Our waterman was a smallish toothless smiling man, shabbily dressed, holding a rafting pole. After we sat down on the deck, clutching our briefcases between upthrust knees, we watched as he shoved off and headed us out into the current. Waving amicably, our hosts went back to the minivan. We were left to the joys of cruising on the Yellow River perched on an antiquarian relic.

For around an hour, we drifted with the current. Since this river is very shallow throughout most of its length, our intrepid captain had no difficulty steering with his pole, gradually angling us over toward the opposite shore. However, the water speed gradually increased and became a bit turbulent. Since our craft was not designed to keep water out, the lower half of our business suits rapidly became soaked through. However, we could give no thought to sartorial matters. We were too concerned about being swept off the open deck, which, by the way, had no railing or safety lines rigged. We did so as we clung to our briefcases, which contained travel tickets and the requisite passports that all foreigners were required to carry while traveling inside China. Our cases also held our currency and critical business documents. By this time, my associate was getting a bit wild-eyed and was muttering obscenities in his native Cantonese.

As the water turbulence reached, at least in our minds, cataract proportions, I nervously looked ahead, fully expecting to see some sort of a spillway. The pilot, however, had already poled us close to the opposite bank. As we passed beneath a large overhanging tree branch, he grabbed a conveniently placed rope that had been previously tied to the branch, hooked his feet to the deck planking, and swung us gently onto the shore. It was obviously a routine maneuver for him, but it was the first time I had ever seen a spring line designed and used in this fashion. A very impressive bit of seamanship . . .

Our local hosts, beaming with pleasure, appeared on the shore from among the trees. It was patently obvious they were quite pleased at having provided their foreign guest with a unique experience. They helped us off our river excursion boat and put us back in the minivan. They had obviously made the trip across the river by a more sensible means—a bridge, and now whisked us off to the railroad station. We said our farewells, and settled down on the train for the passage to our next lecture site . . . dripping wet.

Chinese hospitality . . . Sometimes you just have to "grin and bear it."

Interlude 1

Xi'an Vignette

*—in which a Chinese Muslim criticizes
my tourist approach to shopping.*

Xi'an was formerly known as Chang'an (Eternal Peace). It had served as the western capital for over ten imperial dynasties. During the Tang dynasty (618–906 CE), with two million people Chang'an was the most populous cosmopolitan center in the world. It is the home of the Terracotta Warriors that were buried with Qin Shi Huangdi, the First Emperor of the Qin dynasty (256–206 BCE). The tombs of Tang dynasty royalty, some of which are noteworthy for their below-ground wall paintings showing courtly life, are nearby (about 23 km to the WNW of the city). And, the Big Wild Goose Pagoda, originally constructed in the seventh century, still stands outside the old city wall. Its function was to house the many sacred Buddhist texts that a famous Chinese pilgrim and translator, *Xuan Zang*, collected on a trip to India between 629 and 645 CE, during which he traveled an astonishing some ten thousand miles through Central and South Asia by camel, horse, and on foot.

According to my China logbook (volume #7), I flew from Taiyuan to Xi'an on 1 February 1988. This visit was part of a tour to organize the Trade Risks Seminar in concert with the local CCIC office and Foreign Trade Bureau in each of a number of cities. All my contacts were very keen on the idea, and organizing the details went fairly easily. The major concern of each local CCIC office seemed to be stealing the "cooperative" business we entrusted to other CCIC offices. They had no qualms about invading the turf of their colleagues in neighboring provinces. Side stepping these gambits took a bit of diplomacy, but it was managed.

CCIC's Xi'an staff included three Chinese Muslims, all with the same surname, *Ma*, but not directly related to each other. That surname is common among China's Muslim population. All three of them decided to take me to a unique culinary treat. Picking me up at my hotel at around midnight, we taxied out of the old city through the southern gate in the ancient city wall. There, tucked up against the stones that covered the tamped earth wall structure, was a series of open fire pits over which goat legs were being roasted. The cooks slowly turned the spits and with great deliberation continuously sprinkled various herbs and spices over each leg. Erratic lines of paper lanterns were festooned throughout a grove of linden trees, providing a visual melody line dancing over the *continuo* of the charcoal fires.

We took our seats on wooden benches at a long, rough-hewn log table. Large pitchers of local brew were brought out, which we savored while awaiting our feast. When ready, our roasted goat leg was slung onto the table with a flourish. The protocol for this unique meal was to pull out your pocket-knife, cut off a slice, and consume the delectable morsel without benefit of civilized chopsticks. I was told that this curious culinary custom originated among the Uighur Turks of Xinjiang Province, in China's northwest corner.

Yum! That was one of the tastiest, most memorable meals . . . ever.

In the midst of our convivial chatter, I noticed a Buddhist monk, complete with gray gown and shaven head, walking by us toward the city gate. Tied to his back was a bundle of hand-carved canes, many of them finished and ready for road trials. One particular stick caught my eye. The lower half had been cut to look like bamboo. Above that had been carved a mass of stylized cloud patterns—a design originally found on the cast bronze ritual vessels created during the Shang dynasty (1766?–1027 BCE) of distant antiquity. The handle was a masterful carving of *Shou Xing,* the Chinese God of Longevity with arms extended. (Apparently, being above the clouds, he was "dancing with the stars.")

I jumped up, approached the monk, apologized for intruding, and inquired if he had carved the sticks and if they were for sale. Following his double affirmative response, I asked the price of what looked to me to be a masterpiece of a walking stick. The deal was swiftly concluded, and I returned to my colleagues at the festive board.

After the stick had been handed around for close scrutiny by all, one of my companions asked, "How much did he ask for it?"

I answered, "All he asked for was twelve *kuai.*" (This was less than two dollars in American currency.)

"How much did you pay?"

"I gave him the twelve *kuai* he asked for."

Mr. Ma grimaced, leaned over toward me, punched me in the shoulder and exclaimed, "You should have haggled!"

I honestly did not know how to respond to this criticism. From the Chinese perspective, he was right. It was a matter of "face." I had lost face by not bargaining. My Western viewpoint was based on the assumption that it would have been uncharitable of me to try to lower an already low price offered by a mendicant monk who carved and sold sticks to fill his rice bowl.

Nevertheless, I still use that stick regularly, and feel that I've gotten my two bucks worth out of it.

Chapter VII

The Liberation Standard,
or
From Blue Ant to Pink Bunny

—in which the evolution of the new, more open China is explained in understandable terms; and our market entry strategy gets underway in earnest.

Having traveled and worked continuously all over the China mainland from 1980 to 2004, during which period that country's annual GDP growth was never less than nine-plus percent, it is to be expected that I observed many dramatic changes throughout that country—political and physical, economic and social. The transformation from a "worker's paradise" to a "market economy" is more than a mere terminological shift. China launched itself onto the international stage with intelligence, determination, wary observations, cautious explorations, and no preconceptions. Yes, these developments were a bit messy, even chaotic. That has to be expected in a situation where an entire country was trying to digest in a few short decades the developmental experience that was integral to Western civilization over several centuries. They had a lot to learn.

The explosion of Chinese growth—with new skyscrapers, highways, port expansions, industries, retail chains, and McDonald's restaurants—is documented in academic and economics tomes. Moreover, such exponential growth is too overwhelming for me to do justice to it within the scope of this narrative. Rather, my yardstick for China's reinvention of itself, for its self-launch into the modern world, has more of a symbolic quality. It was the transformation of one person with whom I had regular business dealings from the mid-1980s to the mid-1990s.

Her name was Miss Yang. She was the interpreter-assistant to the CCIC vice president—introduced earlier as the most unabashed plagiarizer of technical and promotional materials I have ever met. Since Miss Yang's boss was responsible for the relationship between CCIC and my inspection company, she was usually my first point of contact when I called at their Beijing offices. It was she whom I most often rang up to arrange meetings for my superiors. I also called upon her to access particular CCIC personnel for operational coordination or problem solving.

At our first meeting in 1986, she was seated in a severely prim manner on the edge of a divan in their conference room with a notebook on her lap. She was dressed in the dark blue uniform associated with China's more ideologically rigid period under Chairman Mao Zedong. Called the "Mao suit" by most Westerners, this high-collared jacket and pants combo is called *Zhong Shan Yi* in Chinese. *Zhong Shan* is a literary style referring to Sun Yat-sen, revered by all Chinese as the Father of the Republic, which was founded after the collapse of the Qing dynasty in 1911. *Yi* simply means garment. The early glimpses into life in China under Mao, in *Time* magazine and elsewhere, often showed huge masses of Chinese workers—all marching in step to Beijing's orders and all wearing this stylistic dress. Their dress stimulated the nickname of "Blue Ants" in the Western press.

Following preliminary greetings, Ms. Yang launched into a forty-five-minute diatribe on the history of foreign aggression in China over the past two hundred years. She made special reference to the vile practice of extraterritoriality, the Opium Wars, the Boxer Rebellion, gunboat diplomacy, and the Taiwan question. This latter was represented as a demonstration of continued interference by America with the internal affairs of the sovereign state of China. Each time I visited CCIC offices, Ms. Yang delivered the same monologue. She always concluded her lecture with a grim reminder of the Law of China that prohibited foreign inspection companies from being established in their sovereign territory. I always listened politely without comment. We would then proceed to discussion of practical matters pertaining to the execution of our cooperative agreement.

Perhaps I should note that this same lecture, or should I say scolding, with minor variations depending on whose office I was in, was delivered by almost all mid-level functionaries I met during the 1980s. Government authorities had obviously standardized the script. It was considered SOP (Standard Operating Procedure) for doing business with foreigners.

With each subsequent meeting over the next couple of years, Miss Yang's obligatory opening lecture got shorter and shorter. Also, her costume started to change. First, the dark blue pants were replaced with a plain blue skirt extending to mid-calf. Then the dark blue, high-necked, long-sleeved jacket was replaced with a plain, long-sleeved, white blouse. Around this time, she announced that since we had been working together for a number of years already, she would be willing to forgo the political tirade completely if I were agreeable to the suggestion. With great seriousness, I assured her that I had it well memorized by now.

By this time, I had made numerous trips throughout China with her boss. We had organized a number of technical seminars and other promotional events, working in cooperation with many CCIC staff. Our meetings took place in Beijing and in various CCIC provincial branch locations. As the face and skylines of the various cities we visited transformed themselves, so did Miss Yang. A-lines, pleats, lace, scarves, earrings, even makeup began to appear with increasing volume and variety.

Ultimately, on the occasion of a joint company tour of port facilities in Hainan, I was flabbergasted at a most unexpected sight. In this tropical island province off China's southern coast and the largest special economic zone in China, Miss Yang wore a chiffon skirt and a pink lace, diaphanous blouse. When we reached San Ya at the southernmost point of Hainan, home of a long beach that rivals Waikiki, she threw off her shoes, ran out onto the pure white sand, and removed her outer garments with gay abandon, revealing a one-piece pink bathing suit underneath. She then proceeded to run into the South China Sea, and splash about with childlike glee.

My other CCIC colleagues continued our conversation without apparent notice, as if that were normal behavior. Whether you call it emancipation or liberation, she had most definitely "come a long way, baby!" The politically reprehensible had become socially acceptable.

Our Cooperation Agreement with CCIC also worked fairly well on the operational level, although all sorts of relationship misunderstandings and fee-sharing problems cropped up regularly. These had to be resolved one-by-one through negotiations. Our ability to serve the needs of our worldwide clientele within the regulatory restrictions relied on our having to undertake these continuous bouts of negotiations. Needless to say, this situation was not satisfactory.

Whereas Miss Yang continued to be my CCIC liaison, as our cooperative activities matured, I developed new contacts and relationships which strengthened over time. China's progressive march toward a market economy was laborious and frequently circuitous, but a cultural shift was increasingly evident. Our corporate strategy for market entry had to be focused on finding a way to alter the legal framework while sustaining a positive working relationship with CCIC. That meant educating China's lawmakers on the place of third-party, *commercial* inspection services in international trade. It also meant finding another potential local partner who would be amenable to the idea of snookering CCIC and its parent unit, CCIB. China's evolving market economy allowed us the freedom of movement to approach other units.

We didn't have far to look. The China State Bureau of Technical Supervision (SBTS), formerly called the State Bureau of Standards, had a large domestic materials inspection function. This inspection function was a part of its role in the creation and publication of technical standards for manufacturing, construction, and consumer safety. While not quite sure what role they might be willing to play in our game plan, I set out to explore where we might be able to establish a mutually beneficial cooperative relationship. This enabled me to cultivate positive relationships with their personnel, as well as get a picture of their political and technical capabilities.

The first thing I learned was that SBTS regarded CCIB's overseer, the State Administration for Import and Export Commodities Inspection (SACI), as bitter rivals. This was most propitious. Over time, I learned that these standards people from SBTS were honest and dedicated professionals. They were more concerned with doing their job well than with playing back room politics. And, they were open to new ideas.

Given our need to maintain effective cooperation with CCIC, I sought a low-level, backburner approach to cooperation with this other bureau. Including them in our technical exchange seminars and conferences seemed reasonable and sensible. This SBTS unit was the obvious candidate for facilitating a strategic flanking maneuver. I therefore found a way to touch base with them on many of my swings through Beijing.

On occasion, I shared discussions on comparative culture with one of the four deputy director-generals of SBTS. He was fascinated with the history of the Jewish people, and he got quite enthused when I introduced him to the newly published Chinese-language version of the *Encyclopedia Judaica*. From that point on, our meetings usually included a discussion of items he found of interest in that tome, along with comparisons of Jewish and Confucian philosophical perspectives. Yes, I said *Confucian*.

Here was another one of those well-educated Chinese, who just happened to be a ranking Chinese Communist Party member, and who had a thorough grounding in his own cultural traditions. His wife later told me that he kept the book I gave him on the table where he ate breakfast every day. She explained that he read an article from it every morning for over two years. One day, she said, her husband closed his book, and exclaimed, "Interesting! All our great Confucian thinkers and all the great Jewish thinkers are teachers!"

There was another shared cultural interest in the case of the mid-level SBTS officials. I am talking about staff members such as their legal officer, their technical review team, and their foreign affairs department crew, with whom I met on a fairly regular basis. We shared a love of northern style hot pots. Our meetings were usually conducted in cheap hot pot restaurants or "greasy chop-sticks," if you will pardon an American-style appellation. These restaurants offered such delights as *shuai yang rou*—thinly shaved and frozen slices of lamb served with vegetables and *doufu* (i.e., bean curd), all of which we cooked ourselves in a hot pot in the middle of our table We consumed our meals with great relish and much beer. The convivial chatter on these occasions provided me with an increasing understanding of some of the more political aspects of the inspection business in China. I also learned that there is a whole world of humorous commentary in Chinese based on the vocabulary and principles of technical standards.

As our organizational relationship developed into something that would eventually produce a major cooperative project, my boss and I began to introduce some of our home office leaders into the mix. This led to formal dinners that were more suitable for senior executives. Given the informal nature of my dealings with these amiable technocrats, my comfort level was high. At one of our first banquets with senior executives in attendance, I actually tried some original humor based on my understanding of the kinds of things this group considered to be funny.

To understand my joke, you will recall that real power in China is based on having control of the Peoples Liberation Army (PLA). One of the major ideological props to the Chinese Communist Party is their being credited with the liberation of China from the evils of foreign aggression. It seemed to me that the word *Liberation* is the Chinese version of *mom and apple pie*. In fact, I doubt if you can find a city in that country of well over a billion people that does not have a street named *Jiefang dalu*, "Liberation Avenue."

So, as we were sitting down at one of our first formal banquets with our SBTS friends, I said, "I think we should eat this meal in full accordance with the *Jiefang biaojun*, the "Liberation Standard."

Everyone at the table looked confused, and then at each other to see if others comprehended my unusual declaration. Then they turned to me for some enlightenment. I explained, "Yes, the *Liberation Standard*! No jackets and no ties."

I suspect the ensuing laughter was more relief that I had not made some sort of major diplomatic blunder than actual appreciation of my joke. Nevertheless, for the duration of my relationship with them, every meal began with somebody referencing the *Liberation Standard*, with much laughter all around on every such occasion. Something as simple as a shared joke proved of great value in cementing the comfort level in what evolved into a complex yet effective relationship.

More importantly, our SBTS friends, over time, were learning that they could relax a bit with foreigners. To me, this was a better yardstick for measuring the effectiveness of the American foreign policy of *engagement* with China than counting the number of new high-rise hotels in their major cities, the rise of per capita income, or a bar chart showing auto sales increases.

In addition, our flanking maneuver had begun . . .

Chapter VIII

Time Out for Some Philosophy,
or
Being Interculturally Competent can be Fun

*—in which the reader must suffer through
my reflective ramblings.*

I recently heard a college professor comment that if you ask ten Americans met randomly on the street to name a Chinese philosopher, at best only three will name Confucius (551–479 BCE). Other than Confucius and maybe Laozi, Chinese philosophers appear sparsely on Western intellectual radar.

Interestingly, the fame of Confucius endured all regime changes in China, eventually propelling widespread recognition across the globe. The names and dates of every one of Confucius' direct descendents have been listed carefully in Chinese historical records, and they've clocked over seventy-five generations. This thinker's ideas—a collage of political philosophy, social commentary, and ethical imperatives—are deeply rooted in the bedrock of Chinese collective psychology. And, those ideas have been used, respected, misused, abused, expanded, revered, twisted, absorbed, adorned, challenged, abandoned, reborn, and transformed over the 2,500 years since he first made teaching a respected profession in East Asia. Confucius lives on.

This is not the place to attempt a synopsis of the vast array of literature stemming from Confucian scholars over the ages. However, there is one rhetorical device that was used quite effectively in Confucian thought, the *chain* discourse. This literary technique builds a framework of cascading ideas designed to lead to, and substantiate, the conclusion. An old English verse, sometimes used by parents to teach a child the idea that actions have consequences, can serve as a simple example.

> For want of a nail, the horseshoe was lost.
> For want of a horseshoe, the horse was lost.
> For want of a horse, the rider was lost.
> For want of a rider, the battle was lost.
> For want of a battle, the kingdom was lost.
> And all for the want of a horseshoe nail.

The prime Chinese usage of this rhetorical tool is recorded in one of the foundational texts of Confucian thought, the *Da Xue* 大學 (Great Learning). Originally a section in one of the early classics on rites and rituals, with authorship traditionally attributed to one of Confucius' disciples, it was selected to be one of the *Si Shu* 四書 (Four Books) by the Confucian scholars of the Song dynasty (960–1279 CE) period. This textual collection of early philosophical works became the core of China's evolving education system. That education system provided a vast administrative bureaucracy for the imperial government through all subsequent dynasties.

A quotation from the *Great Learning* demonstrates how the chain discourse was used. It also shows a Confucian worldview—a core principle that is still discernible when current Chinese leaders expound on "harmony" as a prime societal value. The following version comes from Prof. Derk Bodde's translation of Fung Yu-lan's *A History of Chinese Philosophy*, Princeton University Press, 1952 (p. 362).

> The ancients who wished clearly to exemplify illustrious virtue throughout the world, first ordered well their own states. Wishing to order well their states, they first regulated their families. Wishing to regulate their families, they first cultivated their own persons. Wishing to cultivate their

persons, they first rectified their minds. Wishing to rectify their minds, they first sought for absolute sincerity in their thoughts. Wishing for absolute sincerity in their thoughts, they first extended their knowledge. This extension of knowledge lay in the investigation of things.

Things being investigated, knowledge became complete. Their knowledge being complete, their thoughts became sincere. Their thoughts being sincere, their minds were then rectified. Their minds being rectified, their persons became cultivated. Their persons being cultivated, their families were regulated. Their families being regulated, their states were rightly governed. Their states being rightly governed, the world was at peace.

From the Son of Heaven [the Emperor] down to the common people, all must consider cultivation of the person to be fundamental.

By now you may be asking why this philosophical note is pertinent to my China adventures. Knowing of this touchstone in the Chinese cultural tradition became materially useful during the early stages of my business travels throughout China. This was long before computers facilitated travel arrangements inside that country. In fact, there was no single central office that could arrange for airplane or train tickets with several different internal travel segments. You had to contact directly the local government travel agent in the city you wished to travel from in order to get a ticket to the following stop on your trip. Chinese travel authorities actually recorded reservations by hand on 3"x 5" cards during the early '80s.

On a particular trip in 1982, I was visiting a number of provincial academies of agricultural science. We were negotiating working agreements for the field-testing of a highly selective herbicide that was capable of increasing exponentially the yield per acre of wheat harvests. Departing from Beijing, my first objective was in Xining, Qinghai Province. As I was traveling in rural, agrarian regions, travel involved making arrangements to connect an array of transportation modes. This particular itinerary necessitated a stopover in Lanzhou, Gansu Province, with a change from airplane to train.

Prior to my departure from Beijing, I phoned the government travel office in Lanzhou to ask for a train reservation for my onward travel. They advised that I would be landing at an airport that was located some distance north of the city. They confirmed they would provide a car and driver to meet me upon arrival. Also, I would have to visit their office to pay the fees and pick up my train ticket, after which I would be driven to the train station.

Upon finding their hire car at Lanzhou's airport, I saw that there were two people awaiting me—a driver and an interpreter/escort. She advised me immediately that I would not only be paying for the car and driver, but also for the interpreter's services. I pointed out that I was not advised during my booking call from Beijing that an interpreter would be provided. Nor had I requested one since my command of the language was more than sufficient to find my way about Lanzhou. Keep in mind that this entire conversation was in Chinese. She dismissed my complaint with the comment that she was required to be in the car by "policy." Actually, she was a "minder," whose real job was to watch what I did, note what I said, and report to her "political" supervisor. I thought it a bit amusing that I was required to pay for the government agent whose job was to spy on me.

Here's where I remembered the chain argument. As we started for downtown Lanzhou, there ensued a discussion that went something like this:

> **Me:** I understand that your government has officially approved a three-tiered pricing system for services such as yours. Is this true?

Escort: Actually there are four pricing levels.

Me: Really! Let's see. There's local Chinese, overseas Chinese, and foreigners. Who falls in the fourth tier?

Escort: Japanese. They have to pay even more than the other foreigners.

Me: Really! That's interesting! Well then, I have a question. What if there are two Chinese children who were born in China, but who were taken to America by their parents. Would they get the local Chinese price, or the overseas Chinese price?"

Escort, after thinking a moment: "Since they moved overseas, they would have to pay the overseas Chinese price."

Me: "So, I guess their parents, as parents of overseas Chinese, would also get the overseas Chinese price?"

Escort: "Of course."

Me: "Okay. Then would you please change the invoice for your services from the foreigner's price to the overseas Chinese price."

Escort: "What?! Why?!"

Me: Taking two photos out of my wallet, I said, "Well, if you look at these pictures of my children, you will see that they are Chinese. They were born in China's Taiwan Province, and adopted by my wife and me shortly after they were born. Since by your statement they should be considered overseas Chinese, and that their parents would also be charged as overseas Chinese, then you need to charge me at that rate. I am the father of two overseas Chinese."

Escort: She considered the idea for a moment, and then agreed: "That seems right." And she lowered the price on her invoice.

I knew that arguing against tiered pricing as being inherently unfair, which is what you would expect from an American, would not change the policy. After all, I was on Chinese sovereign territory, and operating within the Chinese cultural milieu, and their rules applied. However, a simple chain argument was readily accepted, and did produce a discount for my company. Simultaneously, social harmony was preserved . . . proving that cultural knowledge (beyond dining customs and ceremonial practices) can stimulate useful insights. It was also an amusing way to deal with an unnecessary, unwanted, but unavoidable service.

In America, conflict resolution and problem solving often utilize confrontation, challenge, and debate. In China, the preferred methods seem to be conciliation, mediation, and diplomatic guidance. However, this does not mean that the Chinese cannot focus on desired objectives within challenging circumstances. I have observed Chinese tactics that would impress a four-star general. While maintaining harmony *a la Confucius* in all forms of interrelationships remains a primary cultural value, the Chinese are certainly aware that conflicts between and among individuals, families, organizations, institutions, regions, and nations are a normal part of reality. This is fully recognized in another early Chinese classical writing, *Sunzi bingfa* 孫子兵法 (Sun Zi's *The Art of War*). One quotation from this text will suffice to demonstrate in prescriptive terms the ideal of successfully handling conflict or competition without disturbing the preferred natural harmony of existence. That is, "Defeating an opponent's forces without fighting is the height of skill."

Written sometime during the fifth to third centuries BCE, Sun Zi's *The Art of War* is a tersely written exposition of military strategies and tactics. These have been studied and analyzed continuously down to today. Not only have the Chinese written many commentaries on, and treatises about, this work, but it is still considered a valuable resource around the world today. This succinct exposition on military strategy is often found in diplomatic circles, military colleges, business schools, and even university liberal arts programs throughout the world. American mythology says that General George Patton, of WWII fame, rode his tank into battle with pearl handled revolvers strapped to his belt and a copy of Sun Zi in his back pocket.

The appeal of this short classic lies primarily in its concise delineation of all the key components for successful management of resources and knowledge to accomplish objectives in the real world. Its principles and practices are applicable beyond military conflict in any kind of adversarial situation, including diplomatic dilemmas, governmental affairs, and commercial development.

Briefly stated, Sun Zi's core strategic principle is indirection; his primary tactical methods involve deception and surprise. The elements of creating successful stratagems are described in terms of intelligence work, logistics, training, and command control. These stratagems are framed within economics, topography, communications, technology, diplomacy, propaganda, and other such points of reference.

Having been hired by the inspection company to help them establish business operations in China, I shaped my agenda with a primary question: How do we change a Chinese law that forbids foreign inspection companies from being established in China? This law was jealously guarded by the Commodities Inspection Administration, and their operational minions in CCIB and CCIC. They held the monopoly over import and export inspections inside China. In considering this problem, I took as my baseline the need to maintain a *Confucian harmony* with all people and institutions involved. I also knew that the success of my employer was reliant upon our capabilities in utilizing the strategies and tactics of this finest mind in Chinese military history, Sun Zi.

This turned out to be the most challenging, the most exciting, and the most rewarding experience in my career as a "shirtsleeve sinologist."

Interlude 2

Roads Less Traveled By

—in which I describe a few "OMG"
a la Chinoise moments.

As the story of my transit at Lanzhou may have indicated, China travel in the 1980s offered some unique experiences. At that time, modern highways and high speed trains had not yet been imagined, five star hotels were still in the distant future, and the internal air passenger transport system was managed by 3"x5" note cards. The best living accommodations available for foreign visitors were called "Friendship Guest Houses." These were cold, dark, and dusty socialist-style leftovers from when China and the Soviet Union were close ideological partners. They were a cultural education in and of themselves.

In the winter of 1981, after checking into the Friendship Guest House in Xining, Qinghai—one of the western provinces, I found myself in the darkest, dirtiest room I've ever experienced. The rug looked like it had not been cleaned since the 1950s. The bed evidently had not been made after the departure of the previous occupant. Moreover, a half empty bottle of *maotai*, the Chinese version of *white lightning*, had been left on the dresser. I won't describe the condition of the bathroom. I confirmed with the guesthouse operator that the previous guest had indeed checked out before I dared contemplating whether or not to open my suitcase.

Before I had even started to unpack, the door crashed open and some kind of a Tibetan tribesman stepped in and stared at me in wide-eyed amazement. Apparently he had never before seen anyone like me. His costume consisted of yak hide boots, baggy pants, embroidered dirty jacket, and one of those furry hats with floppy ear coverings. He even had a large sheathed dagger stuck in the sash that held up his pants. His face was smeared with a thick greasy substance. Perhaps yak butter? I think its purpose may have been to provide some protection from winter winds in the high plains.

He didn't speak Mandarin. I had no idea what language he spoke. Direct communication was impossible. So . . . I picked up the unfinished bottle of *maotai,* and handed it to him with a big smile. A-hah! Human contact had been established! He smiled, waved, and backed out the door—clutching the bottle to his chest. I then locked the door.

That night I utilized another China travel tip. When the room is incredibly dry, fill up the tub, and pour twenty or thirty glasses of water all over the rug. The next morning the rug will be bone dry again, but you will not have dehydrated excessively during the night or wake up with a dry hacking cough.

A month later while transiting Changchun, Jilin Province, in northeast China, my hotel room was not only without heat, but I could get no hot water. And, I really needed a hot bath after a couple of connecting flights all the way from Hong Kong. Upon calling down to the front desk, I received a mind-boggling response. After expressing my need, I was abruptly informed, "There is no hot water in Changchun on Wednesdays." Apparently, this was a fuel cost saving measure by the municipal government. Needless to say, my subsequent trips in and about the Manchurian region were structured to avoid Wednesdays in Changchun.

It was during this period of crisscrossing China to initiate field-testing of that agricultural herbicide mentioned previously that I had to deal with a very tight schedule of meetings with a number of provincial academies of agricultural science. I flew from

Xi'an, Shaanxi Province, and landed in Nanjing, Jiangsu Province. I had a meeting there scheduled for that same day, but also needed to get to Shanghai the following day.

Upon arrival, I immediately went to the local government travel office to ensure my exit. When I asked to buy a ticket, I was told there was only one airplane to Shanghai on the morrow and it was already fully booked. This flight originated in Zhengzhou, Henan Province, and stopped in Nanjing for fueling around mid-afternoon. The agent then said, "We can't give you a seat, but can give you a chair." Being in a rush for my meeting, without thinking I just said, "Great! I'll take the ticket," and whizzed out to make my meeting.

The next day, my kind hosts at the Jiangsu Academy of Agricultural Science escorted me to the tiny airport and we said our farewells. I was the only passenger in the terminal. After a short wait, an old, propeller driven, Russian-made Antonov 24 bounced down on the empty tarmac and lumbered to a stop around three hundred yards away from the terminal building. A fuel tanker started across the tarmac heading toward the aircraft. Following instructions, I walked alone out to the plane, dragging my luggage behind me.

I climbed the gangway, entered the cabin, and saw that all the seats were filled with blue ants, i.e, men wearing the blue Mao suit. I became a little concerned about where I was going to sit. A stewardess came over, checked my ticket, smiled and said, "Please come this way."

The design of this antique vehicle included three spaces in a single line, separated by doors: the piloting compartment, a cargo space, and the passenger seating area. I was led into the cargo area. Cartons of canned food, including sea slugs, were stacked to the overhead on either side of the aisle. The flight attendant said, "Just a moment, please." She left the compartment and returned with a wooden folding chair. A light went on in my head. I now remembered having been told that I couldn't have a seat, but would be given a chair.

Having invited me to sit, my hostess pulled out a piece of rope and proceeded to tie me to the chair. She explained, "I'm sorry that we don't have a proper seat belt for you, but regulations do require that all passengers are fastened to their seats for takeoff and landing."

I was then left alone, tied to a loose folding chair in the aisle, with canned goods stacked up on either side of me. I know what you are now thinking, but I had to get to Shanghai for my next meeting. So, I untied the rope, folded up the chair, shifted the cartons to make a sort of bed, and stretched out for the thirty-minute flight.

And, that's how I flew cargo class to Shanghai.

Around a year or so later, my boss and I had a round of meetings in Xi'an to set up trials of a rubber additive product at a research institute and follow up on our herbicide testing program. Once again, our next stop was Shanghai. Our departure was delayed due to a flight cancellation. Fog can do that in airports not equipped with air traffic control radar. Our hosts moved quickly to ensure that we got space on the next day's flight.

Our plane was another Antonov 24 that had some extra seats installed, making for very uncomfortable leg room. There were eighteen numbered rows of seats in the passenger compartment. Our tickets indicated we were to be seated in row 19. The toilet compartments were located right behind the row labeled 18.

We looked at each other with the unspoken question. My boss said, "No, it can't be." We gave a sigh of relief when the flight attendant told us that due to the added row of seats, the row labeled 18 was really row 19, and invited us to get ready for take off.

Naturally, we joked about narrowly missing flying to Shanghai in toilet class. But then, two more passengers boarded, headed to the rear of the plane, and settled into the two toilets. They had tickets for row 20. During the flight, when anyone needed to use the facilities, they would vacate their seat and wait patiently in the aisle until they could return.

Yup, we just barely missed traveling toilet class to Shanghai . . .

Another trip around the same period provided another sort of experience. Our industrial chemicals department back in the home office decided we should explore the potential market in China for our mining reagents. These were chemicals that had the capability of separating ores out of slurry, i.e., a mixture of water and finely crushed insoluble materials such as copper or zinc. I was told that a team of two mining engineers would handle all aspects of the technical side of the marketing research, but I had to arrange for them to get into a number of mines throughout China.

The Ministry of Metallurgical Industry (MMI) controlled all ore processing for the production of metals. Under MMI's auspices, the China National Minerals and Metals Import and Export Corporation handled all purchases from, and sales to, foreign entities for this particular industry. There were branches of both in every province that had mining and metals production operations. A similar structure handled coal production, with the Ministry of Coal Industry in charge. And, non-metals ore processing, e.g., potash and phosphate, came under the auspices of the Ministry of Chemical Industry's administrative network.

You can see why setting up this marketing exploration trip would prove to be a bit complex. This challenge was further compounded with the location of the mines. They were usually situated in areas which, at that time, were prohibited zones for foreigners. However, the political, commercial, technical and bureaucratic elements of this adventure are not pertinent to the story.

I was able to line up mine visits in Liaoning, Hubei, and Guangdong provinces. I met the two mining engineers who were to be shepherded around China by me after they flew into Hong Kong.

One was a Yankee; the other was South African. Both were the most hard-boiled, hard drinking people I had ever met. They soon led me to understand they belonged to a very exclusive worldwide professional fraternity of approximately three hundred mining engineers of many nationalities who apparently all knew each other. Our trip took around two months to complete. I wasn't accepted as a colleague until about halfway through the trip. This acceptance was demonstrated in a very unusual manner.

Following a technical seminar in Beijing and the first mine visit in Liaoning, we arrived in Wuhan, Hubei Province. This is a river port located over 400 miles up from the mouth of the Yangzi River. Our overnight stay would then be followed by a three-hour bus ride south to Huangshi, a town located 22 km from our destination, the Tonglushan Copper and Iron Mine.

For our overnight in Wuhan, we stayed at the Cui Liu Village Guest House. Its primary guest facility was a small cafe with several Formica topped tables. By this time in our trip, the engineers had discovered a taste for *maotai* with beer chasers. To characterize them further, I would have to say that their linguistic propensities would embarrass the bosun on a tramp steamer. By midnight I could no longer keep my eyes open, and left them chatting away well into the wee hours.

Around three in the morning, there was a loud knock on the door of my room. Cracking the door slightly, I saw a short, rather chunky, fifty-something woman in a gray Mao suit. She shoved the door open farther with the strength of a Russian sailor, and announced that she was from the Wuhan Electric Power Administration. She wanted to discuss a potential joint venture in power generation. Needless to say, it took me quite aback, and some fast talking was imperative to get her out of my room without offending her.

The next day, my traveling companions slyly asked me about my visitor in the night, and did I have any success with initial arrangements for a joint-venture company. Apparently, when she passed the engineers in the lobby, they invited her to have a drink. Discovering she had a reasonable command of English, they then sold her the story that I was the guy to talk to about getting some foreign investment capital. They elaborated that she shouldn't wait until morning because I already had another business meeting scheduled, and gave her my room number. She didn't wait.

Apparently, I now was accepted as an okay guy.

You may find it curious that a middle-aged government worker in the middle of China could speak English back in the early eighties. However, after China's diplomatic rapprochement with the United States, learning English had become a major Party-sanctioned activity, both in and outside all schools. While still in Wuhan, the driver of a taxicab spoke to me in fluent, American accented English. I asked him, "When did you visit America? How long were you there?"

He replied, "No, no. I've never been outside of Wuhan."

I was astonished. "How did you learn to speak such good English?!"

He replied, "The radio. I've been listening to the Voice of America for several years. I do it when my cab is empty."

Another interesting discovery occurred after we arrived at the mine and met the director and his staff. I asked if this mine was in any way connected to the mine of the same name that had been opened around eight hundred years ago during the Southern Song dynasty (1127–1279 CE). I had learned about this mine back when studying the unique, but short-lived, proto-capitalist economic developments in the China of that period. The mine director beamed at me. "It is the very same mine!" He was very proud to be responsible for this still productive part of China's past. Once again, I rediscovered how much Chinese people welcome foreign appreciation of their history. The director went out of his way to be helpful and to answer all our exploratory questions for potential market development.

And then, in June 1983, our industrial chemicals marketing manager and I were asked to explore the possibility of producing our specialty chemical additives for paper manufacturing in China. The business model would be a processing agreement whereby our raw materials would be shipped to a Chinese plant, which would then use our proprietary technology under license to produce the specialty chemicals. Since the shelf life of this product would not permit shipping the end product from the States and across the Pacific Ocean, having a China processing facility would permit expanding sales throughout the East Asia region.

We sailed up the Pearl River from Hong Kong to Guangzhou (*aka* Canton) on a hydrofoil. It was fascinating to be sailing up the river where much of the First Opium War (1839–1842) between Britain and China was fought, and to identify the battle sites. After a round of meetings with the Guangzhou Petrochemical Industries Corporation and several plant visits, it was determined that the best candidate for this project was one of their plants in a place called Jiangmen.

Jiangmen was a small port on the Feng River where it flows into the West River, which was part of a large delta that empties out into the South China Sea. My China logbook vol. #3 has a note stating that the population of the Jiangmen region at that time was around 3.2 million. I was also told by local officials that some 2 million people from the Jiangmen area went to America to work on the cross continental railroad projects in the nineteenth century. Perhaps this explains why there are so many Cantonese restaurants in the U.S.

The business story here involves a three-month negotiation of a confidentiality agreement with the Guangzhou corporation. The idea that Chinese authorities would be required to keep a foreigner's secret from other Chinese authorities was somewhat difficult for them to understand, much less accept. When they finally signed, we were told this was a "first" in Guangdong Province.

There was one other interesting discovery. The plant designated to do the actual production work was primarily concerned that they would be allowed to keep the barrels in which were packaged the raw materials that we would ship to them for processing. Apparently, their biggest profits came from a side business—the resale of barrels to other plants throughout the region. Discussions went more smoothly after we understood the importance of this particular agenda item. Digging out hidden agendas is often a critical part of deal making in China.

However, the travel note I want to describe here was our passage from Guangzhou to Jiangmen. Around eight people were crammed into a small van for the four-hour ride, which included a car ferry crossing of the West River. The road had only two lanes, and was not exactly paved. After a couple of hours jostling along this traffic filled artery, I asked if we could have a pit stop. There were serious intestinal seismic rumblings that needed satisfaction. Given that this was well before the time when McDonald's invaded China, I was not sure how this would be managed. Once we had left the environs of Guangzhou City, I had not seen anything resembling an establishment that might contain a public restroom.

We came to a small village that contained some twenty small concrete dwellings, a bicycle repair shop, and a general goods kiosk. Just beyond the line of houses on our right, the land dropped vertically about 30 or 40 feet to a narrow river that ran parallel to our roadway. We stopped, and I was directed to a small concrete structure that extended out over the riverbed. The platform had four holes in the floor, through which one could look directly into the flowing river. Each hole had a vertical wall on either side, but no roof and no back or front enclosure. Crudely written Chinese characters painted on one of the walls indicated that this indeed was the local loo.

Thinking "when in Rome," I proceeded to get my affairs in

order in that open-air facility. Just as I was thinking about the nice view I had of the river while engaged in that airy convenience, a sampan came into view heading downstream. The front end was piled high with fresh vegetables. Just abaft amidships, a thin, gray-haired grandmotherly woman manipulated a *yuloh,* a long, curved Chinese sweep oar designed to enable forward propulsion as well as steering by one person. She looked up, smiled, and waved in a friendly manner . . . What could I do? I smiled and waved back . . .

Traveling in China continued to provide such amusing discoveries and unexpected cultural consequences throughout my career.

Chapter IX

The Cartography Factor,
or
Institutional Mapping Can Give You
a Sporting Chance of Success

—in which, with due apologies but I have to say this,
the plot thickens.

When China opened up to direct engagement with the international community of economic interests, Western companies seeking a foothold in the new China market had to deal with many political problems. During the first couple of decades, politics trumped economics for the Chinese side when negotiating a business agreement. Oft times the Western business mentality missed this point. Having compared notes with many others involved with China market entry work, I estimated that at least 80 percent of their issues and problems were essentially political in nature. This meant that the guys and gals on the front lines inside China had to study how the political structures were organized and how they functioned in relation to the operational ground of the companies they served. This factor could not be ignored.

The Chinese learned quickly that Westerners loved organizational charts. So they produced them. Their charts showed lots of boxes with both vertical and horizontal connecting lines. They were vaguely accurate in terms of functional reporting links. Unfortunately they did not indicate where decisions were really made or where there were overlapping and conflicting authorities. Moreover, as the Chinese government learned how the international business community worked, their own organizational structures underwent continuous modifications, changes, bifurcations, and mergers. The ground rules were changing in China as the country moved toward the twenty-first century.

However, it was clear then, as it is now, that the ultimate power in China lies along a leadership line running from the Standing Committee of the CCP to the Central Military Commission, supported by the People's Liberation Army. This power focuses on broad, general policies as to the direction of the country. Normally, it does not get involved with the nitty-gritty of how policy is carried out. However, as Kenneth G. Lieberthal pointed out in his introduction to *Bureaucracy, Politics, and Decision-Making in Post-Mao China* (Berkeley: University of California Press, 1992, 8), ". . . authority below the very peak of the Chinese political system is fragmented and disjointed." Professor Lieberthal was not kidding.

Operational reporting lines ran vertically, horizontally, and diagonally on national, provincial, and municipal levels—a kind of three-dimensional matrix management system. Some were political lines, some were functional, and all could be breached using personal lines. Administrative lines and Communist Party lines intersected everywhere on all levels. Underlying these were regional loyalties, school affiliations, family interests, ideological influences, and a variety of other personal commitments and agendas. Anyone who had a social, economic or political agenda needed *guanxi* to navigate a way through this system.

As I saw it, the best way to get a graphic picture of how power and influence tracked within the Chinese government would be to lay on the floor a blowup of the official governmental structure chart. Then, cook up about four or five boxes of spaghetti noodles—*al dente*. Take the strained pasta, get up on a chair, and splash the spaghetti all over the chart. The resultant tangle of noodles will indicate the lines of the flow of power and influence throughout the government. These represent the *guanxi* lines of *personal* connections within, between, and among the various organizational structures. This is what the international community had to map out to be able to understand and manage the environment in which their businesses would operate.

I had some help from my graduate education when dealing with this cartographic chaos. Background knowledge about the structures that evolved historically in Chinese civilization was gained through my study of Chinese political, economic, military, social, and cultural history at Penn. But it was a course at National Taiwan University that crystallized my understanding. We had studied a book by the modern Confucian philosopher and historian Qian Mu 錢穆 (1895–1990), entitled *Zhongguo lidai zhengzhi deshi* 中國歷代政治得失 (A Critical Analysis of Government in Imperial China), Taipei, 1969. This work sketched out and compared the government organizations, civil service examination systems, taxation methods, and defense establishments of five major dynasties over the course of two millennia. Qian also showed how the relationships between the central and provincial governments were managed.

Now, I am certainly not saying that Qian's analysis is directly, or even indirectly, transferrable to the government structure of the People's Republic of China. But the material I studied gave me a framework for understanding China's traditional approaches to dealing with governing a large and well-populated country. It indicated trajectories of operational assumptions, patterns within administrative structures, and social values imbedded in the exercise of sanctioned authority. In many circumstances the communist system in China was very much like the Confucian education and bureaucratic system. For example, Professor Qian stated that throughout China's history it was a generally accepted, even psychologically embedded, concept that the wise and morally worthy senior statesmen and scholars would speak for the benefit of the nation and the people. When the Chinese threw out Confucianism, they in essence were replacing it with Communism as new ideological content in an old mental structure. The idea of an electoral majority representing public opinion just was not in their cultural kit. While it is not beyond the realm of possibility that democracy will eventually evolve in China, the form in which it appears—if it appears—will have a distinctively Chinese twist.

Starting with China National Commodities Inspection Bureau (CCIB) and China National Commodities Inspection Corporation (CCIC), our local "cooperators" for commercial inspection and testing work, I examined the structural connections of their administrating body, the State Administration for Import/Export Commodity Inspection (SACI). A curious bifurcation of authority was discovered within this unit. First, while SACI was considered to be a sub-ministry-level bureau, it apparently had authority to report directly to the State Council. Second, senior executives at SACI were appointed by, and held responsible to, the Party apparatus that was located within the Ministry of Foreign Trade and Economic Cooperation (MOFTEC). This ministry also reported directly to the State Council. Hmm . . .

Apparently, this structural curiosity had an historical origin. CCIB was created in the early stages of the People's Republic as an operational department within one of MOFTEC's earlier incarnations. It was broken out as an independent administration in more recent times. This discovery led to awareness of another significant piece of organizational evolution: MOFTEC had been created by the merger of two previous ministries. One of these prior organizations contained the Party unit that controlled appointments to SACI.

The relationship between SACI and MOFTEC was significant to our interests. While SACI controlled the monopoly on import and export inspections, MOFTEC was the body that put the final stamp of approval on foreign investment projects. These two organizations formed the ground we had to traverse in order to achieve two objectives for successful market entry. First, we needed to find a way to get the PRC Inspection Law changed. This would allow us to establish a business entity legally inside China. SACI and its subordinate units, CCIB and CCIC, would most certainly object strongly to that. They had a powerful influence that could prove lethal to any strategic offensive we might construct. Second, if we succeeded in getting the law changed, we would then need MOFTEC's approval for a business license, dependent, of course, on our finding a Chinese partner willing to work with us in a business venture.

I conducted a number of fact-finding visits to the various departments and divisions in MOFTEC. It gradually came to light that there were strong residual negative feelings between personnel of the two units, which had been merged back in 1982. Fortuitously, one side contained the Party cell which controlled SACI personnel appointments and the other side held the Department of Treaties and Laws, which controlled the approval of foreign-invested business entities. This internal rivalry and division of loyalties would prove useful as events moved forward.

The first bit of luck came during the period in which I traveled with that plagiarizing CCIC vice president described in Chapter VI. During our joint promotional lecture tour beginning in 1988, our program introduced the purpose and value of commercial inspection services to foreign trade, banking, and importing units in the twenty-eight Chinese cities we visited. The feedback from my lectures was positive in every province where we performed. The next step was to leverage the value of our lecture content up into policy-making levels.

I consulted the head of a local communications company we employed in China. The head of this company, Serge Dumont, was an entrepreneur from France. His command of the Chinese language, both spoken and written, had breadth, depth and fluency. In fact, his staff meetings were conducted completely in Chinese. He suggested I chat with the special features editor of *International*

Business Journal (國 際 商 報). She had already attended the *dog-and-pony* show we performed in Beijing, and liked the idea of writing up my lectures in the form of a series of articles for publication.

This newspaper, which had at that time a circulation of around 300,000, was the official journal of MOFTEC. Their distribution list included Party and government administration leaders throughout the country. The editor was very enthusiastic about the idea. Here was a very nice way to start building my own *guanxi* with some of MOFTEC's personnel. I would be providing information about the inspection service industry using a highly regarded and influential media outlet to educate Chinese leaders.

I worked with the feature editor's staff to draft informative material in Chinese that was based on my oral presentations. The end result was the publication of nine articles in late 1989 under the title "How to Avoid Risks in International Trade." (如 何 避 免 國 際 貿 易 風 險). My new working relationship with the editor would be of great assistance in finding my way through the bureaucratic maze inside MOFTEC. In turn, the editor received a plethora of instructive articles aimed at raising the overall quality of the inspection industry in China. That the articles were also valuable as a public introduction to my company was demonstrated by SACI's barely concealable irritation over their appearance.

Seeking to get the maximum promotional benefit from these articles, we put all of them into a booklet. And, the booklet contained the logo of the *International Business Journal.* These booklets were then handed out like Halloween candy at all subsequent promotional events and marketing activities. We published this booklet in large quantities so as to give it widest distribution possible. My editor friend told me that she had convinced a professor at the MOFTEC-administered International Economics and Business School to make our brochure required reading for their students.

By this time, we were well engaged with CCIC in a direct relationship involving a wide range of activities. These activities included promotional, technical, and commercial endeavors. All were very complex in terms of the personal relationships that developed between our respective staffs. This collage of connections with counterparts in their organization provided us with many channels for finding out what was going on inside. We had pinned the center, so to speak.

Of course, our various associates in CCIC also benefited from their relationships with our team. They were receiving an accelerated course of study in contemporary international trade. Learning about the expectations and practices of foreign buyers and sellers gave them new perspectives on competition, which challenged old assumptions about their own authority.

Simultaneously, preparations for our intended flanking maneuver were well underway. You'll recall that we had friends on our backburner, *i.e.,* the State Bureau of Technical Supervision (SBTS). Our objective was to share an agenda with them. They would be ideal partners in a commercial joint venture.

This administrative unit was rapidly developing an expanding portfolio of responsibilities in terms of improving the quality of domestic production. In 1988, SBTS was formed as a vice-ministerial-level bureau by the consolidation of the State Bureau of Standards, the State Bureau of Metrology, and the Department of Quality Inspection of the State Economic Commission. SBTS was then named the Chinese government's official representative to the International Standardization Organization (ISO) based in Switzerland. Other new responsibilities included the administration of China's newly evolving quality certification system, and the establishment and accreditation of national, industrial, provincial, municipal, and county testing facilities. All these connections had potential to benefit both my company, SGS, and the many Chinese organizations charged with developing various aspects of

China's economy. We also verified that SBTS had neither vertical nor horizontal organizational connections to MOFTEC and SACI. They reported only to the State Council's Economics and Trade Commission.

Our relatively modest cooperative projects with this unit, mostly of a technical nature, had gradually risen to a more active level. We organized and escorted some of their fact-finding missions to other standards organizations in Europe and North America. This, of course, gave us the opportunity to show them our facilities in many different countries, and demonstrate how our services were conducted on a commercial basis.

The time had come to push the idea of creating a joint-venture commercial inspection and testing company in China. We told SBTS that this idea was predicated on the State Council being persuaded to see the value of expanding these services into the private sector of China's evolving market economy and changing the Inspection Law to allow it. *SBTS was interested.*

The carrot we offered was the guarantee of a successful business. We had clients all over the world who wanted the risk mitigation of our third-party inspection services when buying Chinese products. We were currently servicing their inspection needs in China through our cooperative agreement with CCIC. These paying customers could be handed to a China-based joint-venture company on a silver platter. Furthermore, we would train the Chinese staff in the various technologies used in providing these services. We also indicated that active marketing of our services to Chinese importers would eventually expand the business even further. All of this would be demonstrated concretely, *i.e.*, by the numbers, in the feasibility study that had to be approved by SBTS before we could begin to negotiate a joint-venture contract.

While the SBTS leadership appreciated what we had to offer, it was obvious they were rather tweaked by the idea of stealing a march on SACI. They would be able to shoulder their way into the import and export inspection business. SACI was clearly viewed as a rival within the SBTS frame of reference. The latter had no hesitation in deciding to create a commercial unit to serve as our potential joint-venture partner.

At that time, already there were many government-owned commercial trade organizations that were controlled by various governmental administrative units. But recently there had been a pullback on government units setting up new commercial entities under their own direct management. Needing an arms-length vehicle for this purpose, SBTS picked a company that it had set up under the auspices of one of its research units. I believe that institute was involved with metrology—developing meters, measuring instruments, and calibrating devices. This was of no significance. Who was actually in charge was all that really mattered. SBTS leaders made all the decisions with regard to how this company was managed.

The SBTS deputy director-general with whom we were working was a native of Hubei Province. Many of his key staff were also from Hubei. The person chosen to be the managing director of the new commercial entity had been plucked out of the Hubei branch of SBTS. Sometimes *guanxi* is quite predictable.

Then, the serendipity factor gave us the opportunity for a diversion—a means of directing SACI's attention away from our activities with SBTS. It came in the form of an idea from an "Old China Hand," an American entrepreneur named John Collins. He had been a member of the Dixie Mission, led by John S. Service of the U.S. State Department, to meet with Mao Zedong and Zhou Enlai in Yan'an in 1944 during WWII. As a result, he had some solid *guanxi* with many of the CCP's old guard, giving him the ability to seek out and obtain support from many of the leaders of China in the 1980s for his business ideas.

By the time we met him, he had created a successful business shipping textile products from Tianjin to the states. He was also a regular client for our inspection services. His idea was to create China's first commercial bonded warehouse in the Port of Tianjin. This would take the form of a joint venture between the Tianjin Port Authority (TPA) and a foreign company that knew how to manage such warehouses. That's where we came in. He approached our company because he was aware that one of our divisions managed a string of bonded warehouses on two continents, Europe and Africa.

A bonded warehouse allows dutiable goods to be landed in a country without the need to pay the customs duties until the purchasing transaction is completed and the goods are ready to be shipped into the hinterland. The actual facility would also house customs officers as part of the security apparatus for the port. The TPA especially liked that part of the project. A rent-free customs office with heating and air conditioning, stocked fridge, cooking facilities, comfortable chairs, TV set, increased cargo throughput, and the foreign warehouse managers handling most of the paperwork—What's not to like?

The idea seemed worthy of serious consideration. A team was put together to look at port conditions and to check out the TPA as a potential partner. We investigated infrastructure, hinterland access, harbor conditions, cargo statistics, and port facilities. Legal review indicated that there was no bar to a foreign investment of this nature.

The TPA seemed very keen on the idea. However, they told us that their office, being a government unit, could not directly invest in a commercial venture. To circumvent this problem, they would have to set up a subsidiary unit that could legally serve as the joint-venture partner. They also explained that since the space occupied by a bonded warehouse was governed legally by the TPA, they had the right to permit our company to operate a cargo inspection unit within the warehouse business structure. That was music to our ears. The only problem was that our warehousing division, based in the Netherlands, was not looking to expand operations. They were not interested in a China operation.

The solution to this hiccup was to offer the project to a very large European shipping firm that maintained a huge warehousing operation worldwide. Our proposal was that in exchange for handing them a unique opportunity to get a foothold in China, we would take a mere five percent stake in the investment. And, oh yes, by the way, we would need a large room on site to house the warehouse's inspection facilities, which we would manage.

Talk about manna from heaven! There we were—moving stealthily toward our own joint venture with SBTS, and now we would be able to hire and start training Chinese staff well before our target operation was up and running.

Warehouse construction was underway when SACI, the Commodities Inspection Administration, discovered our participation in the venture. They went ballistic. Senior officials paraded through the TPA's offices loudly complaining about our participation. They accused the TPA, the shipping company, and us of violating Chinese law, trampling on Chinese sovereignty, and ignoring the authority of SACI and its operational arm, CCIB. They registered a complaint in the local procurator's office. However, their complaint was thrown out. This was not so much because our participation was perfectly legal, but because SACI was playing on the TPA's home turf of Tianjin. Local politics had inadvertently given us an edge. SACI's authority could be trumped by local *guanxi*.

A note on political risk: The warehouse opened just four days before the Tiananmen Square blow up on 4 June 1989. As a result, all our overseas clients who had booked space in the commercial bonded warehouse put a stop order on their shipments to Tianjin. We held our breath for three months, after which foreign businesses started to filter their operations back into China. The warehousing business got off to a slow start, but it grew. The TPA was so pleased with the contribution of this new business to the commercial growth of Tianjin Port that they gradually, over many years, expanded the bonded zone to create a major duty free industrial park.

But for us, Tianjin was a successful diversion. It allowed us to put a few boots on the ground . . . legally. Nevertheless, our primary concern was to change a Chinese law and break a Chinese monopoly. That was yet to come.

Having mentioned Tiananmen Square, permit me a short diversion to comment on my experience on that fateful day. In late May 1989, I was serving as the escort and guide for a ten-man SBTS delegation. We were visiting standards and laboratory certification organizations, both public and private, in several European countries. Naturally, we organized an extensive visit to our corporate headquarters in Geneva, where the hospitality for our guests was offered in a dignified yet warm way.

On the night when the news of the Tiananmen crackdown was broadcast, all of us had just returned to our hotel rooms following a long day of meeting with various technical and marketing divisions at our company's head offices. As the delegation members picked up on this news, they all crowded into my hotel room. All being residents of Beijing, they wanted me to assist them with making international phone calls to their respective families. As each took a turn on the phone, the rest were glued to the television. No one made any comments of a political nature. The collective quiet was broken only by an occasional expression of concerns for family and friends.

I had similar concerns. Two Chinese members of our China Division were also Beijing residents. I first tried to get Mr. Wang on the phone, but no luck. Next, I tried Ms. Ma, who lived in a small apartment not too far from Tiananmen Square. She answered on the first ring.

I said, "Ms. Ma, are you okay? Can you tell me what's happening?"

Ma replied, "I'm all right. I'm hiding under my bed."

A bit disconcerted, I said, "What! Why?"

"There's a big tank parked just outside my window," she answered in a matter-of-fact tone of voice.

"What about Mr. Wang? I tried calling him, but he didn't answer."

'Oh, he's up on the roof with a video camera. He said he wanted to film what was going on."

"Good grief! Is he crazy?!"

Fortunately, all the people we were concerned about came through the crisis without harm. But, it was a very intense experience. These were people I had come to care about.

Chapter X

The Dale Carnegie Factor,
or
The Bottom-up and Top-down Approach

*—in which we move from a really cool strategy
to subtly satisfying tactics.*

I knew from personal experience that foreigners could influence the evolution of the Chinese government's laws, regulations, and protocols in the commercial sphere. For example, back in 1980 when I was part of the team trying to introduce a proprietary herbicide to the PRC Ministry of Agriculture, we asked for copies of their official regulations and procedures for the controlled testing of pesticides and herbicides. The reply was a blank stare. They did not have any. However, they graciously allowed us to introduce the procedures utilized in the States for this purpose. Following careful study of our materials, they allowed us to use them on a *provisional* basis for testing our product in China. It was a learning experience for all of us. Eventually, some of these procedures were incorporated into the testing rules that were formally promulgated by their Ministry of Agriculture.

Given China's lack of an historical foundation in commercial law, whenever it was perceived that commercial regulation was needed in a particular area of concern, study teams were sent on fact-finding missions to learn the relevant laws and regulations in the major developed countries. Eventually there would be a *provisional* law published. Comments and concerns of anyone interested would be entertained and reviewed carefully. The views of foreign governmental and commercial interests would be examined very carefully before making any firm decisions on incorporating parts of them into their own legal guidelines. China's new contract law, intellectual property law, company law, trademarks law, and foreign trade law all evolved in this fashion. It was a tedious process that required much thought and attention to obtaining reams of written documentation that was meticulously translated into Chinese for extensive consideration and review.

However, seeking the modification of an established piece of legislation, as in the case of the *PRC Import and Export Commodities Inspection Law* (promulgated in 1984), required a very different approach. As a foreign commercial organization, we needed to avoid open conflict with a Chinese governmental body that had a vested interest in preserving what we sought to change. We had to develop an effective, but non-confrontational, form of communication to Chinese lawmakers. We needed to provide them with an understanding that there is a substantive difference in both method and purpose between a government-mandated inspection and a commercially contracted inspection of a shipment of goods. And, we needed an *insider* to advocate for a legal change to reflect that difference. At the same time, our company's agenda of acquiring a license for operation had to be kept under wraps. This primary objective had to remain hidden until such time as we could be introduced by a Chinese authority to the highest levels of their government as an authoritative example of that difference between governmental and commercial inspections.

Let me provide context for the situation in which our strategic objective had to work. Winning friends and influencing people in China is necessarily a long-term process. As foreigners, we must generate interest in what we can contribute to China's development, and build their trust in our commitment to that contribution. This must be done at the highest level of their government because all projects and programs of any significance must get their nod of approval. You can build a solid foundation of cooperation and confidence with potential venture partners, but one frown from someone at the State Council level can turn your constructive efforts into a pile of rubble.

Cultivating a local business partner is something that everyone in China operations must work on—from CEO to the men and women doing the work on the ground. That's the **bottom up** work. Keeping this maxim uppermost in everybody's minds, we needed to work positively at every functional level of the target cooperator so that their confidence in our organization was strong at every level. This same work had to be done within the relevant departments of the industrial administrative units, tax departments, planning commissions, land management bureaus, and commercial licensing bodies that had an interest in the commercial venture. If done well, the prospective Chinese partner, and their governing bodies, would be strong advocates inside the system. But this was not enough to have an impact on policy matters relevant to our concerns. Bottom up work must be complimented with top down work.

The **top down** work was also important, possibly more so. But we could not do this directly or alone. People from *outside* our company who were liked and trusted on the highest levels of the Chinese government had to provide the introductions and vouch for our company's value and sincerity. All it would take to kill our China agenda was one State Councilor or a ministerial level Party Secretary to express doubt about the suitability of our project for China's best interests.

We were fairly sure that many of the readers of MOFTEC's *International Business Journal* would have seen at least one or two of the nine articles that explained the purpose and value of third-party commercial inspection. The editor had assured me that all government leaders and departments had subscriptions. But we could not be sure that the key points were noticed, much less understood, by some or all of the relevant State Councilors and their staff. State Council subcommittees dealing with import/ export policies and regulations were particularly important. We needed access in a positive manner to get our message across on the highest levels.

Furthermore, we were also certain that if and when SACI was consulted on inspection matters by State Council staff, SACI would not want to speak very highly of us. They regarded us as a threat to their own best interests. However, they had to be very careful since their operational relationship with us had evolved into a very active "cooperation" in many Chinese ports and provinces. We had pushed hard to make that happen. Now we needed to leverage that relationship to become dynamically visible in Beijing's halls of power. It was time to push the center, and start the flanking maneuver.

To push the center, we needed a highly visible activity that would not only show that we were working coopcratively with the Chinese inspection authorities, but also would attract the interest and participation of high ranking government leaders in the ceremonial aspects of the program. A positive "photo-op" for political leaders everywhere is always an effective carrot. This would provide the access needed to get our key message across to policy decision-makers. And, it would be SACI themselves who would be making the official introductions. No matter how they really felt about us, it would be a public endorsement. At this point in our thinking, the word "snooker"" came to mind. How cool is that?

We had already done several technical seminars with SACI, the Import and Export Commodities Inspection people. For example, in 1987, we organized a rather large symposium focused on American toy safety standards and the related testing requirements and techniques. Toy manufacturing at that time was already a large and growing export industry in several coastal provinces. We brought in representatives of major buyers of Chinese-made consumer products, including such firms as Mattel, Hallmark, and Mitsui to participate in that event. On the Chinese side, factory managers welcomed the opportunity to rub shoulders with representatives of major buyers, and to learn more about how to meet their quality requirements. However, this event was held in southern China, far from Beijing, in the center of China's toy manufacturing region.

Given our success with the toy industry seminar, we decided to replicate the strategy with the textile industry, but this time in the Chinese capital city. In light of the prominent place of the textile industry in China's export trade, we proposed to SACI that we conduct a cooperative symposium in Beijing on textile quality management. Our proposal included plans for massive media coverage. The size and complexity of event planning and preparation was immense, with a task force involving staff from our head office and three subsidiaries, plus a media management consultancy firm.

Our technical and marketing people handled symposium content and roped in the major overseas buyers of textiles as contributing participants. We, the local team, provided the coordinating liaison with SACI, managed the media consultants, handled event management arrangements, and called in the proverbial cards with anyone and everyone in China who could help us get as many as possible senior members of the central government to grace our venues. We got help from friends in the relevant industry and trade ministries and administrations, three foreign embassies, and a number of international trading companies. SBTS, our secret ally, also gave us strong support behind the scenes after we explained our strategic objective.

However, the elegance of our plan was that SACI themselves would be the ones to work the hardest to elevate the public importance of the program. As one of the official hosts, they promoted it as a major contribution to the growth of China's exports since the international participants were all buyers or potential buyers of Chinese products. In fact, they exerted much effort to increase the program's visibility in the highest circles of the central government. And, when they arranged formal meetings with key dignitaries and decision-makers, they took our company leaders along for the *show-and-tell*. SACI had no choice but to vouch for our credentials as a world leader in the import/export inspection and testing business. It was clear to all that we had brought in the international buyers. Throughout the long days and nights of intense preparatory work on this project, I smiled to myself the whole time.

During the month in which the textile quality symposium occurred, May 1988, we succeeded in meeting with three important players in China's power structure. First, the aforementioned major American buyer of textiles, who was well liked and trusted in Beijing, hosted a small dinner party. The primary guest was Mdm. Chen Muhua (1921–2011). At that time, she was a member of the Central Committee of the Chinese Communist Party, a member of the Standing Committee of the National Peoples Congress, and president of the Executive Committee of the All-China Women's Federation. Her previous roles included leading positions in various units responsible for China's economic development. She later went on to become a vice premier of China. Other dignitaries around the table included the acting vice chairman of the Standing Committee of the National Peoples Congress, the head of the Ministry of Textiles Industry, a senior advisor in the Ministry of Public Health, a senior advisor on foreign affairs in the Shanghai Municipal Government, the director of Beijing Hospital (my knot-tying buddy), and the director-general of SACI. Without going into the background of these guests and their relevance to our interests, suffice it to say that the head of SACI was impressed at the assemblage that accepted our invitation.

The next day, SACI's director-general took our leadership group to an audience with Wang Zhen (1908–1993), who was vice chairman of the CCP Central Advisory Committee, and the newly appointed vice president of China. He was one of the octogenarians called the "Eight Elders," who held substantial power in China during the 1980s and 1990s. He was a hard-line communist ideologue who fought bitterly against political and cultural liberalization. However, he was a moderate on questions of economic policy and supported moving China on the path of market-oriented reforms. My knot-tying medical friend had suggested it might be a good idea to introduce Vice President Wang to the idea that a foreign commercial inspection company would give foreign buyers more confidence in purchasing Chinese products. This would ensure he would not object when it came time for the State Council to consider the idea of allowing foreign commercial inspection companies to set up operations inside China.

This meeting, held in the Great Hall of the People next to Tiananmen Square, was followed by a banquet for some ninety administrative-bureau-level VIPs and their staffs. The festivities were hosted jointly by our firm and SACI, although it should be noted that we paid the entire bill. Nevertheless, by now it was well established in governmental and foreign trade circles that SACI had effectively vouched for us as a competent and respected working partner.

Our final ceremonial visit brought us into the *Ziguangge*, the grand hall in which foreign dignitaries were met during the last imperial dynasty. This hall is located inside a section of the Forbidden City called *Zhongnanhai*, which serves as the inner sanctum of the Party leaders—the headquarters of both the CCP and the State Council. The Chinese use the term *Zhongnanhai* in the same manner as Americans use the term *White House, i.e.,* a reference to the seat of power.

It was here that we met with Bo Yibo (1908–2007), who was another one of the "Eight Elders." Previously having served as a deputy prime minister, and chairman of the State Economic Commission, he was now vice chairman of the CCP Central Advisory Commission. Once again, we were introduced by the director-general of SACI, and had opportunity to clarify how a company such as ours differed fundamentally from CCIB, SACI's operational arm, and how we could help promote Chinese exports.

As a side note, each of us in our entourage was graciously granted the privilege of having our individual photographs taken with Bo Yibo. The one of me became a potent defensive weapon at a later stage in our growth. But that story must be put on the backburner for the moment, and will be told at the proper time in this narrative.

At this point, we pushed our allies, SBTS, to continue the battle inside the State Council. The *PRC Import and Export Inspection Law,* along with several other foreign trade laws, had been tabled for review and possible modification around that time. SBTS's objective was to have the old prohibition of foreign inspection companies from being established in China tossed out of the revised statute. They already knew that we were firmly committed to establishing a joint venture with them, provided that the nasty one-line prohibition was expunged from the law.

We were now engaged on a variety of fronts. The traveling trade risks seminar, in cooperation with CCIC, was in full swing. Technical quality control seminars, also in cooperation with CCIC, continued to be organized in various production centers along the China coast. Marketing calls were being made at the government-owned import and export corporations. Actual inspection work on behalf of our international clients was being carried out under the euphemism of "technical exchange" with CCIC, which received partial payment of the inspection fees for their "services." And, the joint-venture commercial-bonded warehouse company in Tianjin was under construction and scheduled to open in early summer 1989.

So, even before the warehouse opened, which event caused SACI to react like a bombshell had exploded in their garden compound, we commenced mobilizing our flanking maneuver. Negotiations for a joint-venture inspection and testing company contract with a business entity under the auspices of our main ally, SBTS, had begun.

Interlude 3

Stopping Crime Can Be a Marketing Tool

*—in which my Chinese working partner
executes a stroke of genius.*

During this period of rather intense activity, I was working very closely with a valued colleague, Denny Mak. He came up with a brilliant idea for promoting our inspection services in China. A Hong Kong native, his Mandarin was infused with an accent derived from his native Cantonese language that was thicker than Hungarian goulash. He had a tremendous work ethic. The only thing I had to be concerned about was his tendency to lose all energy at noon if he was not sitting down for lunch. In fact, when we bashed about China together on business trips, I always stashed an emergency supply of packaged snacks for those occasions when our morning meetings ran a bit long. As long as he was fueled properly, his high productivity was marked by a dynamic creativity and good humor. It was a great partnership for exploring the frontiers of commercial activity. I must say that working with someone you like and respect is one of the greatest pleasures in a business career. I liked and respected Denny Mak.

Denny's marketing idea was based on the nature of how international purchasing transactions were subject to criminal fraud. Allow me to explain. When a buyer in China wants to obtain fishmeal from Chile, or machinery from Italy, or grain from America, he will negotiate a purchasing contract with the overseas seller. This contract will specify the quantity and quality of the product, price and packaging requirements, shipping details, and payment terms and conditions. Unless the buyer and seller have had a long-term relationship built upon mutual trust, the seller normally required the buyer to open a Letter-of-Credit (LC) with a bank.

In the China of the 1980s and 1990s, Chinese importers used the Bank of China for this purpose of establishing an LC. This meant that the buyer would deposit the amount of the purchase price with the bank, under the condition that the bank could release the money only to the seller, and only *after* the bank received proof that all the conditions of the sale were fulfilled, including delivery of the cargo per contract terms. The conditions of proof were specified as certain shipping, insurance and inspection documents.

The inspection certificate would be issued by an independent, third-party inspection company. They were entrusted with performing a preshipment inspection, usually ex-factory or at port of loading, depending on the nature of the cargo. The inspection company's job was to verify that the commodity shipped conformed, or did not conform, to the quantity and quality stipulated in the purchase contract. For example, there was one occasion in the late '80s in which a television manufacturer in Guangdong Province sold a container load of color TVs to a buyer in Indonesia. Just before the container was loaded on board a freighter in Hong Kong, one of our inspectors discovered that the cargo consisted entirely of black-and-white TVs, with a market value much less than what the buyer had agreed to. Our inspection certificate noted this discrepancy, and when sent to the Indonesian bank holding the buyer's LC, the bank stopped the release of funds to the seller. The buyer was pleased that the planned rip-off was thwarted.

However, there was a weakness in this system. The bank holding the LC was not legally required to *verify* that the documents they received were valid. A dishonest exporter could ship product that was not the contractually agreed quantity and/or quality, send a falsified inspection certificate to the bank along with all the other requisite documents, and walk away with the money. If we had not been specified, and officially notified, to do a preshipment inspection on that TV shipment, the seller would have been able to snooker the buyer.

My partner's idea was to approach the various branches of the Bank of China and ask if they had ever been defrauded by releasing importer's funds on the basis of a spurious inspection certificate. We rapidly discovered that the answer was a uniform and resounding "Yes!" wherever we went. In every visit, the bank manager hauled out a huge stack of forged documents that had caused major losses to Chinese importers. They were all frustrated by their inability to prevent these crimes. They did not have the expertise to distinguish between real and phony documents. Even though it was not a legal requirement, they recognized that it would be a great service to their customers, and to their country's economic development, if they had a way to make a quick check on the validity of the certificates submitted to them.

Denny's idea was elegant. Our company had a worldwide network of inspection facilities. Our operational methodology already involved regular communications with any branch that was commissioned to perform a pre-shipment inspection on China-bound cargos. If the Bank of China required Chinese buyers to stipulate in their purchasing contracts, not merely a third-party preshipment inspection, but specifically an inspection by our company—by name, our local office would verify the validity of any dubious inspection certificate that landed on their desks. The bank's only cost for this service would be for sending us a fax copy of the questionable document. We would then contact the branch named in the certificate and ask them to confirm whether or not they had performed the inspection and issued that particular certificate. A quick phone call back to the bank resolved the question.

And, more proactively, if the buyer were instructed by the bank to send our local office a copy of the purchase contract that stipulated our performance of the preshipment contract, we would pass that information along to the relevant overseas branch. That way we could make sure our inspectors would be standing on the dock when their cargo was scheduled to be loaded on the vessel. This was a valuable service because some sellers would not call our local offices when we were named in the purchase contract, but rather forge one of our certificates and forward a phony report to the Chinese bank.

Our various branches worldwide would willingly participate in this program because they had a vested interest in eliminating fraudulent certificates. The Bank of China would gain kudos from their clientele. And, our company would increase its business volume because of the resulting increased demand for our services.

Eliminating crime became a valuable marketing tool. As the various branches of the Bank of China came to appreciate this *gratis* service, they became increasingly proactive in persuading Chinese importers to agree to stipulate our company by name in their purchasing contracts and/or LC terms and conditions. With one simple little service, we had turned a Chinese banking network into an extension of our marketing team. This did, however, give us occasion to be embarrassed by the bank's enthusiastic support of our program.

For example, on one occasion I received a phone call from one of our major international clients, a New York City-based dealer in minerals and metals. He wanted to know why our company's inspection certificate had been stipulated in a purchasing contract with a Liaoning Province minerals exporter with whom he had a long-term relationship of proven mutual trust. In this case, both seller and buyer had been trading for many years and had decided that independent third-party cargo inspections were no longer necessary. Subsequent investigation discovered a clerk in the Dalian branch of the Bank of China whose job was to generate the requisite LC documentation. Denny Mak had met with him on one of his marketing trips and had sold him on the idea of our free inspection certificate verification service. Apparently, this clerk had arbitrarily and independently added the unnecessary clause requiring our company's inspection certification as part of the transactional documents without advising either buyer or seller. We sorted out this hiccup quickly, and considered ourselves lucky that our New York client had a sense of humor.

The long-term benefit of Denny's idea was a process that introduced our services favorably to more potential Chinese customers. The creation of a new ally, the Bank of China, was another facet of the bottom-up work.

Chapter XI

The Documentation Factor,
or
Corporate Lawyers Have Good Reason
to Be Nervous

*—in which a Big Cheese from the home office learns
how negotiations in China are a bit different
from negotiations in Switzerland.*

Differences in cultural viewpoints between Westerners and Chinese can be seen in their respective attitudes toward a contractual agreement. In the West, businessmen expect a contract to delineate all relevant responsibilities and obligations for each party, as well as the specific objectives of the business arrangement. The terms and conditions of the dissolution of the agreement are also spelled out in great detail so as to reduce costs and guard respective proprietary interests as much as possible if and when business cooperation is no longer possible for whatever reason. This makes for lengthy contractual documentation before any aspects of the intended business cooperation is undertaken.

On the other hand, Chinese businessmen seemed quite comfortable with a one-page agreement, with few written concrete details about the cooperative business arrangement. To them, this document merely memorialized the initiation of a cooperation in which all matters and interests are subject to infinite renegotiation. It indicated the creation of a new relationship *a la Chinoises*. Thus, as business cooperation progressed, those who agreed to work together would engage in ongoing talks to address and resolve arising business concerns. Moreover, for example, the Chinese deputy general manager of a Sino-foreign joint venture would have no qualms about asking the foreign general manager to write a letter of recommendation for his piano playing daughter who has applied to enter the Julliard School of Music. And, he fully expects a well-written letter, even if the foreigner is tone deaf, and doesn't know the difference between Chopin and Scott Joplin.

This contrast in cultural presuppositions was amply demonstrated when the time came for us to negotiate a joint-venture contract with a subsidiary of the State Bureau of Technical Supervision (SBTS). These negotiations took nine months to reach a successful conclusion. In the late 1980s, that was considered a comparatively rapid timeframe between beginning and concluding a joint-venture contract in China. While I could take satisfaction in retrospect, at the time of these negotiations there was some external stress added to the usual suspense of coming to a mutually satisfactory contractual deal. Our negotiations had to be done furtively so as to avoid detection by SACI, the Import and Export Commodities Inspection people. The actual sit down discussions took place in a lengthy series of laborious sessions in a smoke filled conference room in one of the older Beijing hotels. This venue was deemed less likely to attract the notice of SACI than it would if our negotiating team marched regularly in and out of SBTS's headquarters building over a period of nine months.

Prior to this point of joint-venture contract negotiations, our cooperative activities with SBTS had been increasing steadily both in volume and complexity. During 1989–1990 we organized a number of overseas fact-finding missions for some of their staff. These missions included facilitating their contact with other national standards organizations, the testing laboratories and accreditation authorities of these national organizations, as well as visits to our own subsidiaries. These overseas visits were vital for their understanding of how a commercial inspection and testing facility functioned, which would help them grasp better the reasons behind some of the complexities we would be introducing during the joint-venture contract negotiations.

SBTS's major job, which had been ongoing ever since China decided to open up to the West, was the elimination of the old system of product quality production standards, which they had copied from the Soviet Union. Their objective was to adopt over time, industry by industry, the quality standards established by the International Standards Organization (ISO), based in Switzerland. Without going into all the dry-as-dust details, suffice it to say this was a monumental technical and educational exercise that would eventually have a deep effect on the evolution of China's economic reform program. The enormity and intensity of SBTS's work to adopt quality standards for Chinese production served as working background knowledge for SBTS leadership to understand the value of commercial inspections.

SBTS also seemed to understand how to deal with interests of a more political nature. In 1988, they greatly expanded their role by absorbing national-level bureaus in related fields, *i.e.,* metrology and quality supervision. We were, therefore, not surprised when they accomplished the objective of eliminating the prohibition of foreign inspection and testing companies being established in China. With the promulgation of the revised Inspection Law by the National Peoples Congress, SACI's monopoly over import and export inspections was broken. Now our joint-venture negotiations could get underway in earnest. You will forgive me for a sincere "Amen" at this juncture. Our bottom up and top down communications strategy had required widespread coordination and intense focus, but our efforts were successful.

The unit chosen to be our joint-venture partner was called the China Standards Technology Development Corporation (CSTDC). Officially, it was a commercial entity established under the auspices of a national metrology research institute. SBTS was the official administrator of the institute. This created a sort of arms-length hands-off position for SBTS *vis-à-vis* this corporation. The arrangement was stimulated by a recent State Council directive requiring government administrative units to cease and desist from directly running for-profit commercial organizations.

The general manager of CSTDC was a career bureaucrat from SBTS's Hubei Province branch. He was an old friend and classmate of the SBTS deputy director-general who was in charge of supervising the working arrangements with our company. CSTDC's business activities at that time involved primarily organizing expositions, both in China and overseas. The expositions were for the promotion and sales of Chinese manufactured meters and instruments that were used in a multitude of industries.

As the weeks of negotiations with our CSTDC counterpart took place in the smoke-filled hotel rooms, there were many points of disagreement and even conflict in our discussions. Most of them were solved by patient and respectful explanation of the relevant commercial and/or legal background. Lunching together on a regular basis facilitated increasing mutual trust. Occasionally, some really sticky items were taken upstairs to the SBTS deputy director-general who, together with one of our senior managers, would take the role of arbitrators. Fortunately, the key SBTS arbitrator was the guy who liked to discuss Jewish history and culture with me. Nonetheless we would sometimes organize field trips to one of our branch offices for a bit of *show-and-tell* on how our business was organized. This tactic often helped to clarify how to resolve needs on both sides of the negotiation table.

Another useful aid came from a local Chinese law firm. We had hired this firm to assist us on the recommendation of the MOFTEC journal editor with whom I had worked on that series of articles about avoiding trade risks. Our home office legal department questioned the rationale for this expense. This is an example of the cross-cultural home office problem that was not uncommon to on-the-ground point men for China market entry. I had to provide a rationale that would not impugn the quality and capabilities of our home office legal staff while communicating the need to employ local culture resources. In this particular case, I had the good fortune to report that this firm was run by two former members of MOFTEC's Department of Laws and Regulations. This was the very department that would have the final say on whether or not our contract would be approved under the newly revised Chinese law. This connection would prove extremely useful in what followed.

The men and women of this local Chinese law firm were helpful in three ways. First, before we tabled a draft article for inclusion with the draft contract, it would be floated by these legal advisors who would let us know if it would be acceptable to their former MOFTEC colleagues. Second, we had them meet often with our prospective business partners to assist with explaining the purpose and value of some of the items that their negotiators had questioned. And, third, they kept their former colleagues in MOFTEC apprised of the progress and content of our negotiations. This latter activity was a critical part of our plan, given the likelihood of a strong negative reaction from SACI and their political allies when they discovered what we were doing with SBTS.

When we submitted the signed contract for MOFTEC's approval and issuance of our business license, we wanted the bureaucratic wait time to be as short as possible. The idea was to complete the process before the other half of MOFTEC, *i.e.,* the side with strong ties to SACI, found out about our contract. The plan worked, and we received contract approval before the political storm broke—but just barely.

However, before getting to that part of our adventure, I want to explicate what was involved with our actual contract negotiations. We had a checklist of items for inclusion, along with drafts for each clause. Our approach followed the old precept that if you want someone to eat a whole pie, it's probably easier to feed it to them one slice at a time. Some of the items, such as the definition of key terms and the scope of business, were not problematical to our prospective business partners in terms of acceptability. On the other hand, there were times when discussions slowed down. Two notable slow downs came as we proceeded through management structure and headed toward arbitration of disputes and the conditions and method for dissolving the company.

Explaining the many points needed for creating a solid contractual foundation for the joint-venture company required not just patience, but also sensitivity to possible misapprehensions on the other side of the negotiating table. Getting in all the items required by our legal department without appearing dictatorial required diplomatic skills. They were very sensitive to any apparent inequalities in our relationship. Occasionally, frustrations would boil over into anger. On one occasion during the lengthy explanations of the reasons for a detailed plan for closing the company, their lead negotiator flared up. In an exasperated voice, he exclaimed, "We're here to arrange a marriage, and we haven't even kissed yet, but all you talk about is a divorce!" The explosion of laughter on both sides broke the tension, but we still had to take the time to assure him that our concerns were based on sound commercial reasoning. Much of that reasoning was discussed rather extensively outside the negotiating room—at lunches, dinners, and visits to cultural sites such as the Summer Palace, the Temple of Heaven, the Great Wall, the Ming Tombs, the Forbidden City, and Liulichang, a district where antiques were sold. We definitely needed a lot of breaks from that smoke filled room.

As noted earlier, there also were difficulties reaching a harmonious understanding with our own legal watchdogs. This was a fairly common phenomenon. In fact, I've often heard people in the field who served other transnational companies refer to their own headquarters legal staff as "deal killers." This was a concern that worried me because our home office had recently hired a new legal department chief. He was an experienced, battle-hardened corporate lawyer, who came to us from a senior position in a multinational chemicals company. After one month on the job at corporate headquarters in Geneva, he was told about the ongoing negotiations in China and was asked to review our progress.

Our legal chief noticed that our working draft contract did not contain a service mark protection clause. This was clearly an oversight on the part of our negotiating team. Our service mark on an inspection certificate or testing report was the mark of trust in both civil and criminal courts worldwide. And that reality was part of our competitive edge in international trade. That trust ensured customer loyalty. However, at that time China's Trademark Law did not contain service mark protection. Thus, our contract had to create the necessary protection.

Our new legal eagle flew to Beijing with the text he wanted in our contract. After social preliminaries at our hotel, he showed me the draft service mark protection clause. I thought, "Oy!" It seemed longer than our entire draft containing all the other clauses, from Terminology to Arbitration.

That first evening we sat in the hotel lobby. After coffee was served, I asked if I could tell him a story about an earlier negotiation—one that had occurred in the early 1980s back when I worked for a transnational chemicals corporation. Given his own background with a chemicals manufacturer, he showed interest. This is what I told him.

The company I used to work for wanted to sell in China its proprietary technology for the production of a chemical product that had many industrial applications. Preliminary inquiries made among relevant Chinese production and trade organizations eventually resulted in some interest. A small team of marketing and technical people was organized, and off we went to meet the prospective buyers in Beijing. Introducing the technology was a lengthy process, but we eventually got to the stage where a draft technology purchase contract reached the negotiating table.

The representatives of China's technology import authorities already knew that Westerners put a great deal of words into their draft contracts. In typical Chinese fashion, however, they tried their best to reduce both the number and length of the various clauses and conditions. They were uncomfortable about writing down so many details.

There were other problems, too. When we came to the arbitration clause, they wanted the venue to be China, and we were told by our corporate legal department to make it America. The argument went on for several days. We were accused of disrespect toward the Chinese judiciary, and that we were looking for an unfair advantage in case arbitration became necessary. The fact that China had not yet set up its own international arbitration body was considered irrelevant.

I forget who came up with the idea, but the impasse was resolved by the suggestion that since China was in Asia, and the United States was in North America, perhaps it would be acceptable to both parties to choose an arbitration body located in Europe, a kind of third-party court. We settled on Sweden, *i.e.,* the Stockholm arbitration rules. But now we needed home office approval, and a draft clause for the contract.

My boss, the head of our team, knew our legal department chief personally, and was able to explain to him by phone our negotiating problem. The legal czar, whose eye patch and bald head made him look very much like Moshe Dayan, decided Sweden was perfectly acceptable. He said he would have his staff draft appropriate wording. Furthermore, since it was a fairly standard clause, he would have them telex the text directly to us as soon as possible.

The next morning, a telex was delivered by hotel staff. Single-spaced and typed in all caps, our newly drafted arbitration clause was almost three feet long! My boss looked at it with dismay and said, "This will go in the Guinness Book of Records." Calling the legal department boss again, he complained that the telexed document was longer than the entire draft contract plus one of the appendices.

The response was, "Wait a minute 'til I get the file."

We waited. When he returned, he laughed. "No problem. The first paragraph says what's necessary. The rest is merely a rather elaborate statement of the content of the Stockholm protocols. I thought this would be a simple exercise for my staff and didn't see the need to check it. I'll sort them out. I'm happy with just the first paragraph."

My boss happily responded, "Great!" He then turned to me and said, "This is what I want you to do at tomorrow's meeting . . ."

The next day, after we all settled in with our ritual tea at the negotiation table, per my instructions I announced that we had received the draft arbitration clause by telex, stood up on a chair, held the rolled up document over my head, and let all three feet unroll. The reaction from the Chinese team was a loud, "Waaaaaaa." The dismay at the prospect of reviewing the entire text, not to mention getting it translated into Chinese, was palpable.

I then said, "May I make a suggestion?" Whipping out a pair of scissors, I cut off all the text below the first paragraph, letting it fall to the floor. "How about if we just use the first paragraph?" After the applause and laughter subsided, the first paragraph was unanimously accepted with minimal discussion.

My boss grinned from-ear-to-ear right through lunch.

At the conclusion of my tale, our top lawyer thought for a moment, and then asked, "Are you telling me I should reduce the length of this clause?"

I replied, "Although a bit of textual consolidation would be appreciated by the translation team, I understand the need for this item. I just have to come up with a non-confrontational way to present it. They are very sensitive to any appearance of inequality. The point of my chemicals story was that sometimes when dealing with the Chinese we need to find a creative way of introducing an idea that may be outside their frame of reference, outside their experience."

The corporate lawyer asked, "What possible objection could they have to the protection of our service mark?"

I responded, "They probably have no idea of the commercial, much less legal, significance of a service mark. The sheer length of this clause will make them uncomfortable. And, by presenting such a long clause we might stimulate the subcutaneous xenophobia that some of the older Chinese still have if there are suspicions of an untrustworthy motive. I've seen that happen before in other Sino-foreign negotiations. If they get the idea that we're trying to gain an unfair advantage and cheat them out of something, the whole deal could *go south*."

"So, what do you suggest we do? That clause must go in." Our legal eagle was adamant.

After taking a moment to think, I suggested, "Let me take your draft to the business center here in the hotel. I want to make another copy, replacing our name wherever it appears with their company name. We'll table this copy first tomorrow, taking all the time necessary to teach them why *they* need service mark protection for their own company. This will take a while because they'll be digesting a totally new concept. Once they agree, we'll say, 'Oh, yes. We'll need the same clause with the exact same wording for our company, too.' "

It took me several hours to retype the clause. It took several days to spoon feed the lesson on this particular international business practice to the Chinese side. At first they objected to a long clause about something that was meaningless to them. They argued that their company was relatively new and the scope of business services was still evolving.

We asked, "What if ten years from now your company has become a strong industrial player and you need legal protection

against imitators?" They were not impressed by *legal* consider-
ations. They expressed a commonly held Chinese view that the
possibility of becoming ensnared by their own court system was
something to be avoided. Nevertheless, the explanation of the
rationale for service mark protection was an educational opportunity. And later, SBTS would become an ally in support of the
passing of China's service mark protection law by the National
Peoples Congress.

We then shifted cultural gears—away from the legal aspects,
and explained that a protected service mark was an important part
of the "face" of the company. The final step was to take a break,
take our lawyer to the Wangfujing shopping district, and come
back to the negotiating table a couple of days later. As I explained
to our corporate lawyer, we had to allow the real lead negotiators, the ones behind the scenes whom we never saw, to mull over
our explanations and documentation. They would make the final
decision. The tactic worked very nicely. They accepted the clause,
and had no difficulty understanding that our own transnational
business required the same protection.

Our lawyer went back to the home office with new appreciation
of our work *in the field*.

Chapter XII

Chinese Law,
or
A Wedge or a Sledge?

—in which the evil Empire Strikes Back,
after which things get really nasty.

The tenets of Western culture have been framed with an historical bulwark of jurisprudence having a foundation of reasoning
and logic as evidenced in the Socratic Method. In contrast, the
leaders of traditional China espoused their vision of creating an
ideal social order through moral suasion. There was a code of
generally accepted norms of behavior. The canon of Confucian literature, which contained all the fundamental elements of this code,
provided the tools for educating the governmental administrators
of Chinese society.

Interestingly, there was no codification of commercial law in
China's pre-modern historical period. Social disputes were normally arbitrated by scholars trained in the Confucian classics. On
the other hand, criminal law and civil statutes were promulgated
by the rulers in the successive imperial dynastic governments.

After 1978, as China moved toward a market economy, foreign approaches to the regulation of commerce were studied and
analyzed. This was followed by publication of temporary "provisional" laws for experimental application. Further review of how
they actually worked in the evolving market economy would ultimately result in modification, approval, and official promulgation.
These could be revisited by the legislators should serious problems
or concerns justify revision.

However, there was a serious flaw in the process of creating workable commercial guidelines through the legislative and administrative processes. Specifically, implementation required a major educational effort. Announcing a law was one thing. Getting China's large bureaucracy and its budding business community to understand and accept legal requirements for the conduct of commerce was another. It would require a seismic cultural shift. Nevertheless, this circumstance had a significant effect on the success of our market entry strategy. We now had the law on our side to open a foreign commercial inspection company. We also had internal allies who endorsed the positive outcomes on China's trade that would be derived through commercial inspections. Despite this, we still faced hurdles because application of the law was in its infancy. Moreover, SACI was a formidable organization with powerful influence in each regional market.

Sometimes, SACI's power was reflected in a unique manner. For example, when the State Council ordered all governmental units to divest themselves of direct control over, and financial interest in, commercial entities, SACI was exempted. They were allowed to retain direct control over their commercial unit, CCIC. On the other hand, SBTS had placed their commercial unit, our joint-venture partner, under the auspices of a separate research institute. They also made it clear that any distribution of joint-venture profits would be retained by the respective joint-venture partner firms. Furthermore, the Tianjin Port Authority also had picked a commercial unit in which they had no financial interest to be the partner in our joint-venture commercial bonded warehouse.

But SACI was not required to divest its interest in CCIC. All profits from CCIC operations continued to go directly into the coffers of SACI. Therefore, we were not surprised that SACI decided to ignore the change in the Inspection Law that gave our joint venture legal status.

SACI chose to ignore the revised Inspection Law's elimination of the barrier to foreign inspection companies being established in China. They continued to assert that we could have no legal standing in their country. They continued to play the old game of claiming that they held an "internal directive" that maintained the standing prohibition. Of course, we were not allowed to see this internal directive because it was "classified" under the State Secrets Act. This was a common power game played by many officials throughout the governmental bureaucracy at this time in China's history.

Then, when SACI got the news that we had successfully negotiated a new full service inspection and testing Sino-foreign joint-venture company with an SBTS unit, and had just been officially approved by MOFTEC (in September 1990), they went berserk. I mean they really flipped out. Since the next step in the bureaucratic process involved registration of the business with the State Administration for Industry and Commerce, SACI attacked there first. Going to the office in charge of reviewing our application for registration of a business license, SACI filed a brief that was filled with wildly false allegations of corrupt and criminal actions on the part of our company. SACI was throwing every foul thing they could think of to get the Industry and Commerce Administration to disapprove our application.

There ensued a battle royal inside the department handling our application that eventually revealed internal corruption in the form of bribery and intimidation. As a matter of due process, that department had notified SBTS, as the initial approving body for the new joint venture, of the charges that had been lodged by SACI. Fortunately, our friends at SBTS had their own strong allies inside the Industry and Commerce Administration. SBTS was able to set in motion a criminal investigation that stopped the attempt to prevent official registration of the new company. One bureaucratic career in the corrupted department was interrupted by her sojourn in prison as a direct result of this battle.

With the ultimately successful registration of the joint venture's business license, our management team got to work setting up headquarters in Beijing and our first branch office in Shanghai. Hiring and training staff got underway. The entire inspection staff employed by the Tianjin bonded warehouse company became employees of the joint venture. These aspects of setting our business in motion were not difficult because of the groundwork we had laid while implementing our market entry strategy. But that didn't mean we were finally out of the woods.

SACI was not done with trying to destroy our fledgling business. Their smear campaign was redirected toward their contacts in the National Peoples Congress and in the State Council. Their formidable stature as a well-known State organization translated into their ability to gain access to the highest PRC decision makers. They embarked on their own flanking maneuver. Their maneuver had to be countered by our own high level friends who could access directly vice premiers, state councilors, and other senior Party leaders and set the record straight. Naturally, SBTS took a major role in this process. One of my friends in SBTS confided that their long-term objective was to absorb SACI, and that having the law on their side in this battle served their purposes on several levels. Self-interest is a great motivator.

While counterattacks were going on at the highest levels of PRC government about the efficacy of foreign joint ventures for commercial inspection, SACI also took advantage of having the official brief to carry out the new Inspection Law. In October 1990, SACI wrote and published that law's Implementing Regulations in which they gave themselves the authority to approve and accredit the work of all inspection agencies in China. This was a very creative interpretation of the Inspection Law, which actually made no mention whatsoever about commercial inspection companies, foreign or domestic.

Twisting and supplementing the authorized text of these

regulations, SACI created an extralegal rationale for revoking our business license. They claimed our license was not valid because we had not applied for, nor received, SACI's approval. Our joint-venture partner took the lead in fighting off this attack. One thing to look for in a Chinese partner is political savvy and political clout. We were happy that our joint-venture partner had both.

The joint-venture management focused on growing the business. Within five years this new company had ten operational branch offices, five testing laboratories, and over one thousand locally hired staff. It achieved an operating profit in its first full calendar year of business. The next years were even better.

Meanwhile, SACI and its CCIB/CCIC minions continued to focus their efforts on disrupting and destroying our business. Our informants inside CCIB told us that one of SACI's several deputy director-generals created a ten-man attack squad whose only purpose was to destroy our new joint venture. Their tactics included the following:

Threatening to withhold export license approvals from Chinese companies that allowed foreign inspection companies to inspect their export products.

Circulating "internal directives" to provincial foreign trade departments and companies engaged in export industries falsely claiming that our joint venture was engaged in illegal activities in China.

Intimidating our inspection staff in the field with threats of arrest and blocking their access to factory inspection sites.

Colluding with port officials and local State Security Police to obstruct access to port facilities by our inspection staff.

Attempting to persuade both national and local level governmental authorities that our approved business scope was illegal under the terms of SACI's rather creative interpretation of China's Inspection Law, as documented in the Implementing Regulations they wrote and published.

Clearly, they saw laws and regulations as a sledgehammer. For example, SACI was the publisher of the official "List of Import and Export Commodities Subject to Legal Inspection." This list itemized products subject to mandatory inspections by CCIB for the purpose of protecting the "public interest." It was their major source of funding since they held authority to charge Chinese importers and exporters with fees for their inspection services. The original list consisted of 148 imported products and 333 export products. Shortly after the new Inspection Law went into effect, SACI came out with a new list, increasing the number import commodities to over 300 and export items to over 500. The new list included almost every significant product in China's foreign trade, and SACI controlled the import and export licensing approval process for all the items on this list. Their list became a weapon to support their threats—another sledgehammer.

Not content with an expansion of mandatory inspections, other forms of skullduggery were applied. The particulars of one of SACI's attacks should give you a taste of the environment in which our fledging company was operating. As indicated in the old English *chain* discourse recorded in Chapter VIII, a small detail in preparations can have disastrous consequences. The "nail" in this case gave SACI an opportunity to attempt preventing the issuance of the annual renewal of our business license in the third year of its existence. We were caught off balance.

One of the staff on the SACI attack squad assigned with the task of destroying our joint venture must have assiduously examined the paperwork documenting its formation. This SACI staff member discovered that the Scope of Business stated in the business license approved by the Industry and Commerce people differed in wording from the wording in the *initial* approval document issued by MOFTEC. Actually, we had spotted the error immediately, and a corrected approval document had been issued, but SACI put a creative spin on the correction.

At SACI's instigation, in September 1993, two investigators from the procurator's office of the Xicheng District in Beijing visited the joint venture's main office unannounced. They stated they were looking into "a charge" that the joint venture's management had paid a bribe to the official reviewing their license application to "change the Scope of Business on their license." They also wanted to know why we had not applied for review and registration with SACI, claiming that this was a legal requirement under the new Inspection Law's Implementing Regulations.

Naturally, this accusation of having committed bribery was vehemently denied. And, the investigators were also told that registration with SACI was never required by any of the approving bodies during the initial process of applying for contract approval and a business license. Nor was it required by the Inspection Law itself. In fact, our MOFTEC-connected legal counsel had confirmed to us that SACI was not part of the official regulatory protocol for obtaining approval for a joint-venture contract. This was a matter for MOFTEC and the Industry and Commerce Administration only. Our joint-venture staff explained this patiently and meticulously to the two visiting investigators.

To ensure that honest and clear communication was taking place, one of the original board directors of the joint venture, an SBTS legal officer who had handled the contract approval process, visited the procurator's office. We desperately needed to find out just what in blue blazes was going on. I had post-event interviews with the SBTS officer and the joint-venture staff member who accompanied him so as to report back to our regional managing director and recommend further action. My subsequent written report had this explanation: "During this visit, the investigators showed him a copy of the first approval document issued by MOFTEC which contained a scope of business different from that on the business license issued by the Industry and Commerce Administration. The SBTS officer, Mr. Liu, explained that the first approval document had been subsequently annulled by MOFTEC and when it was discovered that both the name of the company and the scope were incorrect, a second [corrected] approval document was issued." The investigators wanted documentary proof.

We then contacted the Beijing law firm that had assisted us with the joint-venture contract negotiations and asked their view of the situation. They advised that since the investigators did not show any document from the procurator's office authorizing an investigation, none of our staff were obligated to talk to them. They added, "However, friendly cooperation is usually the best policy in such situations." This made us more uncomfortable. Lacking an *independent* judiciary, China's entire legal apparatus was something to be avoided like a tailgating 18-wheeler going 80 miles per hour down the Jersey Turnpike in a blizzard. Both the Chinese and the foreign sides of our partnership were of one mind in this regard.

In Mr. Liu's second visit to the procurator's office, a representative of the Beijing Municipal High Court was present. This dignitary claimed that he was there merely to "observe and assist." The investigators stated that their main concern was to determine whether or not the licensing department official who issued our initial business license had received a bribe from any of the joint venture's officers. We were instructed to prepare a full written report on our actions in this regard, with accompanying relevant documentation.

We immediately called a meeting of SBTS officers, joint-venture staff, and our Beijing lawyers to thrash out the form and content of this report. They worked well into the night. The next day, my chief assistant, Mr. Wang, delivered the report. Three days later, we got a phone call from his older sister, who worked for the BBC. She told us that on the previous day the authorities had asked Mr. Wang to come in for "some further clarifications." A day later, he still had not returned. Apparently, he had been detained for questioning. Things were now getting really messy.

His sister and one of our staff camped out at the procurator's office, demanding that he be released. While our incarcerated team member was Chinese and had been born in Harbin in the far northeastern corner of China, he had Australian citizenship, which he obtained when he was a university student in Sydney. Therefore, we notified the Australian Embassy of the situation and asked if they could assist. At their request, I provided Embassy officials with a full briefing, including the background story of our complex relationship with SACI, CCIB, and CCIC. They agreed to join the protest posse.

An Australian consular officer showed up very quickly and demanded the release of their citizen. When the Chinese investigators refused, he explained their situation in diplomatic terms. Per Australia's consular treaty with China, now that their embassy had taken official notice of the situation, the Procuratorate had only 48 hours to hold him without charge. After that, a formal complaint would be registered with the Chinese Ministry of Foreign Affairs. The consular officer added that even if their citizen was required for further questioning, he must be allowed to return home in the evening. He must not be held over night as he was on the previous day. The consular officer later told me over obligatory post-crisis beers that he had no authority to say that, but decided to "wing it" before things went any further. (I have always liked Aussies, and their style.)

While this action ultimately got our guy out of detainment, we soon learned the reason why the Beijing High Court had sent an "observer." When SACI lodged their complaint against us with the Xicheng District Procuratorate, they simultaneously lodged a complaint with the Beijing Municipal High Court about one of the joint venture's recent inspections on a cargo being shipped out of Shanghai. The shipment was some heavy machinery sold by the Shaanxi Branch of the China National Machinery Import and Export Corporation to an Indonesian buyer. This machinery was used to produce something called "floating glass." To this day I have no idea what floating glass is, or why anyone would want to produce it. Nevertheless, apparently this particular design of machinery was, according to SACI, an official state secret. They accordingly charged us with *high treason* because we had inspected this cargo without any proper authorization to do so.

We went into emergency action mode, *aka* panic stations. We needed to determine what the heck this inspection was all about. Yikes! Chinese state secrets and accusations of treason were a viciously virulent combination. This was bureaucratic *blitzkrieg* in spades.

Upon reviewing the inspection report and accompanying shipping documents, it turned out that our inspection mandate had been to check only the packaging. Inspectors had checked that the shipment containers had not been breached and had been properly sealed. They also verified that the labeling on the outside of the containers was correct per the shipment documents. Our inspectors had not actually looked inside the boxes and had not seen the cargo itself. We also could not resist pointing out that if this product was an official state secret, why in blue blazes were they selling it to the Indonesians?

We gave copies of all the relevant documentation on this shipment to the SBTS deputy director-general who volunteered to speak directly to the Beijing High Court on our behalf. This was my Chinese acquaintance who had been steadfastly reading the Chinese-language version of the *Encyclopedia Judaica* for a few years already. He told me to contact our Beijing lawyers and get them geared up to initiate court action against the Industry and Commerce crowd should they issue an injunction to stop all our business activities on instructions from the High Court. I acted on his advice with alacrity. Fortunately such a suit did not prove necessary. SBTS then made a formal complaint against SACI for an administrative protocol violation. SACI had not informed SBTS, as the joint venture's primary approving body, of the charges they had made—as was required by administrative protocols. Our evidence proved sufficient to have all charges dropped. I suspect that our SBTS protector had some useful *guanxi* inside the High Court.

SBTS really stepped up to the plate on behalf of the joint venture during the attack on our business license renewal. Their leaders eventually reported on SACI's political machinations, legal tricks, and false accusations all the way up to the State Council and the National Peoples Congress. They were truly committed to our defense. I have a note in my records for 1994 that states: "When Ms. Ma hand-delivered a copy of our (renewed) license registration to SBTS, they broke out a bottle of some local booze in celebration. Ms. Ma came back to the (Beijing) office a little tipsy from the experience."

These attacks appeared in various places, in various forms, at various times. For example, in early 1994, a Hong Kong based company invited me to participate in a conference they were organizing. I was asked to make a presentation on "The Development of the Inspection Business in China." Shortly after I agreed to their request, I received a letter withdrawing their invitation. The letter stated, "It has been brought to our attention that there is a court case pending in the PRC involving [your company, and] it has deterred a number of other potential speakers from participating in our conference." The letter concluded with a retraction of the invitation "to speak at this time."

This was a crock of bull. My company was not involved in *any* litigation in China. A simple inquiry with the conference organizers uncovered that this false allegation had been made by the Hong Kong branch of CCIC. Nonetheless, they were nervous about the possibility of having a confrontation with an arm of the Beijing government. We trumped CCIC by arranging to import a speaker from SBTS's legal department, who confirmed in this public forum that our company was not involved in any litigation, and reconfirmed the legitimacy of our joint venture's status in China.

As we expanded to other port cities, harassment followed. On one occasion in Qingdao, Shandong Province, our inspectors had spent several days checking the contents of export shipments at a freight container yard, and putting our company's numbered seals on each locked container door. The purpose of the seal was to confirm that the container contents matched our inspection results on the date of inspection. If any seal was found broken upon arrival at the destination port, the shipping company would bear the legal liability for any damaged or missing cargo. After the last day of these inspections, staff from the local CCIB office showed up at the yard in the evening and broke all the seals, apparently using 5 lb sledge hammers. They were observed and identified, but our complaint to the local authorities went nowhere. Apparently, *guanxi* had trumped legalities.

In Dalian, the local CCIB colluded with Customs agents at the entrance to the harbor area to keep our inspectors out. Even worse, CCIB staff kept showing up at our branch office to harangue our staff with charges of illegal activities. It was at this point that I remembered the photograph taken of me standing next to Bo Yibo, one of the "Eight Elders," in the main formal greeting hall in *Zhongnanhai,* the seat of power in Beijing. Vice Chairman Bo's son, Bo Xilai (1949–), was the current mayor of Dalian. The serendipity factor was in play again.

Digging the photo out of my files, I had it framed and took it with me on my next trip to Dalian. Arriving at the joint venture's branch office, I listened to the complaints and concerns of our staff. I then asked for a hammer and nail, and hung the photo prominently in the reception room. Once the regular CCIB troublemakers observed the photo, their visits to our office ceased. Apparently, they decided a bit of restraint was in order if one of the joint venture's board members had been endorsed by the mayor's old man.

We also invited the director of the Dalian Port Authority, along with some of his key staff, to a dinner. While the discussion centered primarily on what he was doing to compete with the port of Tianjin for shipping traffic, we did manage to mention some of the "paperwork difficulties" our Dalian branch office staff were having. That problem disappeared completely within two days. Port access was no longer a problem.

Throughout this period of attacks in every possible location, SACI made a critical error. Their mistake was to make each attack in succession, *i.e.,* one by one. With our limited personnel resources to counter these attacks, their sequential approach allowed us to counter each one as they occurred. If they had tried to execute three or four of their plots at once, we would have been hard put to defend against all of them simultaneously.

Of course, we did not win every skirmish. Early in 1994, SBTS's Policy and Legislation Department chief asked me to provide him with a "Problem Briefing Report" in which I was to describe examples of SACI's attack campaign that had occurred over the past two years. My report was rather long. One entry will suffice to show CCIB's technique.

I wrote in my report, "In November 1993, inspection staff went to Fangchang, Guangxi Province, to carry out a commercially entrusted inspection on some steel products that had been discharged in that port. Local CCIB officials prevented our staff from carrying out the inspection, claiming that it was illegal for us to do inspections in China. They then said that our inspection would be permitted if we paid them HK$20,000—cash up front." That amount in Hong Kong dollars would convert to around US$2,600. Real subtle! Our inspectors returned without carrying out the inspection.

Our thin on-the-ground staffing was evident in how we had to manage inspections that sometimes required specialized knowledge and expertise in a particular product area. Given the wide variety of products we were called upon to inspect, *e.g.*, machinery, grain, electronics, iron ore, textiles, crude oil, toys, steel, etc., our inspection capabilities required a wide range of technical skills. Specialized staff was often borrowed from company subsidiaries in other countries for both training and inspection work.

On one such occasion, the Shanghai branch of the joint venture borrowed a technician from our Philippines subsidiary. CCIC's Shanghai branch somehow learned about his arrival, and forcibly incarcerated him in his hotel room shortly after he checked in. They refused to release him until one of our managers negotiated an agreement by which CCIC would receive a cut of the fee that was being paid by the foreign buyer for the inspection and inspection report.

Our young Chinese inspection staff were often confused and upset by CCIB's machinations. However, by taking the time to sit down with them in small groups and explain the full history of our complex relationship with SACI and its operational arms, CCIB and CCIC, they became willing scouts who would let me know when CCIB was pulling some new skullduggery.

Throughout all these problems, SACI continued to tell false tales about our activities in China to senior government officials. SBTS worked to defend the joint venture, but it is difficult to counter a slanderous whisper campaign under any circumstances. I would have to come up with an additional strategy as a counteroffensive to the onslaught of SACI attacks that seemed never ending.

Here's where I remembered something I learned from a friend in Beijing. While the Communist Party made sure that uncomplimentary articles about China did not appear in the Chinese media, the Party leaders wanted to be aware of anything negative about China that appeared in the international press. They handled this by creating a top-secret newsletter that contained translations of such reports gleaned from all over the world.

This journal was called *Neibu Cankao* (內 部 参 考), which translates as "Internal Reference." Actually, it was my understanding that there were two such papers. One had a circulation of around 300; the other around 700. Naturally, there was no way I could obtain their distribution list, but I could be sure that everyone in the Party's Central Committee and the State Council would be on it. It would be a violation of the state secrecy act for me to obtain a copy of this journal. However, the mere knowledge of its existence gave me an idea.

I wrote an article in English about the feuding within China's inspection bureaucracy, including much of what I've written here about the abuse of authority. I then approached one of the editors of the most prestigious journal that specializes in the analysis of China's evolving economic system and business environment, *The China Business Review.* Explaining that I did not want to be identified because of possible repercussions against my company, I asked if they would consider publication of my article under a pseudonym. After reviewing my draft, they agreed. It came out in the May-June 1993 issue of *The China Business Review* under the title "Inspection Turf Wars." The next step was to translate the article into Chinese, and arrange for both the original English version and the translation to be delivered (by my friend in Beijing) to one of the researchers who worked on the *Internal Reference* journal's staff. I was advised that the article was published shortly thereafter. Around two months later, a senior official in SBTS told me that SACI's malicious slander campaign on State Council level had subsided. I suspect somebody got his hand slapped. It's nice when a plan actually produces the intended outcome.

Then, in 1993, the National People's Congress passed a law that was nothing less than the proverbial *manna from heaven.* The serendipity factor was at work again. Called the "Anti-Unfair Competition Law," Article 7 stated, "Governments and their subordinate departments may not abuse their administrative powers by restricting other parties to purchasing the products of their designated business operators or by restricting the fair business activities of other business operators." SACI was clearly engaged in activities that violated this law.

However, how could we call them to account? Taking SACI to court was not an option. A private company with a foreign joint-venture partner suing a Chinese government agency would be the height of folly. China does not have an independent judiciary. Hard evidence would not be able to counter insider influence.

We decided to copy one of SACI's tactics. They were handing out copies of their self-written "Inspection Law Implementing Regulations" to every enterprise visited by their inspectors, claiming that those rules proved that our joint venture was operating illegally. So, we had our inspectors hand out copies of the new Anti-Unfair Competition Law when they went out on inspections. We highlighted Article 7 to bring attention to the proof that SACI/CCIB was engaged in illegal acts by virtue of its propaganda campaign and coercive tactics.

We also worked closely with our Beijing lawyers—the ones who were former officials in MOFTEC's Laws and Treaties Department—to prepare an opinion paper on their letterhead which confirmed the legality of our joint-venture's operations inside China. This letter was in the form of a response to a series of questions raised by the joint venture's management. The questions were based on the assertions about our illegality which SACI had put into an "internal directive" circulated to all Chinese exporters. It took about one week for our joint committee to craft the form and content of the letter.

Copies of this legal opinion letter were distributed to the trade together with copies of the Anti-Unfair Competition Law. The joint venture's inspectors were also instructed to mention that the legal opinion letter had been written by Beijing lawyers who had previously worked for MOFTEC. The implication of such a connection was readily understood by all.

We targeted not only Chinese trading and manufacturing companies, but also hit our international clientele who did business with these Chinese units. This was necessarily a slow process, but it gradually had a positive effect. We were using Chinese law as a wedge, levering SACI's influence away from our business.

Early in 1994, we discovered that SACI had persuaded the commercial counselor in the PRC Embassy in Indonesia to issue an official protest to the Jakarta government that our China joint-venture was performing illegal inspections on cargoes being shipped to Indonesia. This gambit was serious because our inspections on these particular cargoes represented a very large slice of our business. Our subsidiary in Indonesia was able to obtain copies of the letter of protest. We passed the letter on to SBTS. They in turn fired a formal complaint directly to the State Council, accusing SACI of violating the Anti-Unfair Competition Law. We also took one of SBTS's legal eagles to Jakarta for the purpose of defending the legality of our China joint venture. He was very successful in countering SACI's influence inside the PRC Embassy.

The head of SBTS's legal department told me that the timing on this action was perfect. Apparently, the State Council was in the final stages of preparing a series of internal directives that would redefine the structure and function of all governmental ministries, administrations and bureaus. Without going into the technicalities of Chinese bureaucratic terminology, suffice it to say that after these internal directives were finalized, SBTS had expanded its sphere of authority in the quality assurance service industry, as well as put a larger umbrella of legal protection over our joint venture. It was a very nice result of some nasty political infighting.

We were not the only target of SACI's hit squad. For example, my records contain a memo dated February 1994 in which I reported that one of our competitors—an American-based electronics testing company had recently tried to set up a joint venture in Xiamen, an island port in Fujian Province. I wrote that this laboratory "signed a joint-venture contract with 'Fujian Province Product Quality Supervision and Inspection Institute' earlier in 1993." Since this institute came under the auspices of SBTS, I learned from my sources inside the latter that after the contract received provincial-level approval and the initial capital outlay was deposited in a local bank, the project was shot down by SACI head office interference when the contract was submitted to the Industry and Commerce Administration for registration and licensing. Apparently, a SACI deputy director-general and the governor of Fujian Province had a close personal relationship. *Guanxi* trumped legality, again.

I have to admit that we did not win every skirmish. In early 1995, a representative of the Hong Kong branch of SINOCHEM, China's official agency for importing and exporting chemicals, visited my company's Hong Kong office with a special request. His office had been handling international transactions on behalf of production units in Jiangsu Province, and was frustrated with CCIB's lack of technical capabilities in Zhanjiang, a port on the lower reaches of the Yangzi River. Apparently, their inspection and testing reports on petrochemicals were proving grossly inaccurate. Evidently, the consequences of these erroneous reports included some sort of penalty fees, as well as trading disruptions. He wanted one of our specialists to organize a seminar on petrochemicals inspection and testing technology for CCIB's staff in Zhanjiang. We provided him with the resume of our designated senior technical specialist in this area, and both his office and the people in Zhanjiang agreed to host the seminar. However, at the eleventh hour, the CCIB Commissioner for Jiangsu Province learned that our expert was also the general manager of our Beijing-based joint venture, and killed the seminar. Nevertheless, the joint venture was firmly established, despite continued harassment from SACI/CCIB.

The feud between SACI and SBTS also went on for several more years. For example, in 1995 the negotiating team in charge of China's bid for accession to the World Trade Organization (WTO) was led by senior MOFTEC officials. This delegation included SACI leaders who were there supposedly to deal with the technical aspects of some of the non-tariff trade barrier issues. The problem here was that given SACI's narrow function, *i.e.*, government-mandated import and export inspections on a published list of commodities, they were not qualified to discuss issues related to national technical standards, metrology, and domestic product quality. That was SBTS's turf. However, despite the latter's position as China's official representative to the International Standards Organization (ISO), International Electrotechnical Commission (IEC), and other such standards bodies, SBTS asserted that they had been excluded from the WTO negotiating team as a direct result of MOFTEC and SACI's opposition to their participation.

However, their feud subsided some years later when SBTS managed to absorb SACI into their own administration.

I love a happy ending . . .

Interlude 4
Cross-Cultural Adjustments

—in which more "OMG" moments
are exposed.

The board chairman of the new joint-venture was also the general manager of China Standards Technology Development Corporation (CSTDC), our joint-venture partner company. I was named one of the board directors of the joint venture, with the understanding that my primary function in this role was to serve as the communications link with the chairman, who did not speak English. Another part of my responsibilities here was that of a watchdog. Under Chinese law, the chairman of a joint venture is the "legal representative" of the enterprise. This meant that his signature (or rather his "chop") could bind the joint venture to legal commitments without any authorization from the rest of the board. Discovering what the chairman might do on his own without due consultation with the foreign partner was a delicate intelligence job.

Our joint-venture chairman wanted two of his own staff appointed to the joint venture's management team. As the general manager would be an experienced operations executive from our Hong Kong based inspection company, one of the chairman's staff was to serve as deputy general manager. His primary function was to shadow the general manager and learn how to run a commercial inspection business. The other appointee was an aged bookkeeper, who had experience with Chinese bank procedures, Chinese tax reporting, and other such fiscally related matters. Including these two staff made good sense to us for both the start-up and the long-term development of our joint venture.

After operations were underway for a while, the general manager became uncomfortable when he examined the books. This young British gentleman was well experienced through his previous position as the head of one of our largest departments in our Hong Kong subsidiary. He asked to borrow the chief accountant from the Hong Kong office and have him examine the joint venture's financial records. After a few days at it, our accountant informed us that Chinese currency was being moved from CSTDC into the joint venture and being exchanged for U.S. dollars. The U.S. dollars were then being transferred from the joint venture's bank account to an account in Hong Kong owned by CSTDC. Both of these actions violated Chinese law. This practice of using the new joint venture to exchange Chinese currency from another company into U.S. currency did not affect the profitability of the joint venture. However, Chinese currency was tightly controlled by the government, and there were specific facilities, regulations, and procedures for foreign exchange transactions. Nonetheless, the venture's chairman stated correctly that CSTDC was not stealing any money from the joint venture. He asserted that since our two parent companies were partners we should not object to allowing this small "convenience" for CSTDC.

Yikes!

The negotiations over this peccadillo on the part of our partner were as difficult as they were delicate. Being the board member with the responsibility of monitoring the board chairman, I orchestrated a meeting with him, the joint venture's management team, and the finance manager from the Hong Kong subsidiary. After a diplomatically difficult discussion, we finally enabled our chairman to see the light by showing him (a) the article in the contract that called for an annual audit of our books by an independent and local accounting service which would be obligated to report any illegal practices to the authorities, (b) the regulation allowing the local Tax Department to check our books at any time, and (c) the prevailing statutes making those specific transactions and transfers a criminal transgression. We resolved his problem by guiding him through the legal facilities that the government had set up to manage currency exchange.

As I said, "Yikes!"

With the passing of this early crisis, a new episodic situation emerged from the chairman's office. After the first half year of operations, one of our Australian inspectors was sent to Beijing to help out with some specialized inspections and training. The joint venture's chairman called him into his office, along with an interpreter, and asked him to transmit a message to me. The Aussie didn't know it, but he was being drafted into the position of a Chinese-style middleman.

The message was straightforward. He, the chairman, now realized that the joint venture was part of a worldwide operational network with a worldwide reputation of trustworthiness. Therefore, in the interests of properly representing the dignity of this major service system, he would need a Rolls Royce or Cadillac. Would our home office make this purchase for his use in Beijing?

Using a middleman, instead of talking directly to me on my next swing through Beijing, was the means of asking without the loss of face if I had to deliver a negative reply. I arrived in Beijing about two days after the Australian left Beijing on a job. Even though I had already received the message, neither I nor the chairman mentioned the latter's request. It was strictly business-as-usual.

After proceeding to the next stop on my trip, I contacted the Australian and asked that he transmit my reply to the chairman. I told him to say that because we were a service company, any display of opulence or extravagance in our offices or our facilities, including vehicles, would cause our clientele to think we were extremely wealthy and probably overcharging them. This would cause us to lose customers. Because of this, our home office had strict policy guidelines that prevented such a purchase. The Australian had a bit of difficulty accepting the idea that he *had* to be the one delivering my reply. I accordingly gave him the lecture on the culture of the middleman in China.

On my next trip to Beijing, the chairman and I took some time out to visit the National Military Museum. We had a pleasant stroll through the exhibits, examining artifacts from replicas of ancient Song dynasty siege weapons to WWII artillery. It was a full day of convivial conversations. Our exchange via the middleman was never mentioned.

While the episode of the car request was resolved relatively easily, everyday management of the joint venture brought an entirely new way of life for the general manager. Our British general manager had to function through an interpreter. Learning Chinese while simultaneously running a start up business in China is not impossible, but it is certainly extremely difficult. The job required long hours, including weekends. As a result, he was continuously dependent on a translator to communicate with those around him, and he had little opportunity to seek out Westerners for conversational conviviality. No wonder he welcomed my periodic visits to his offices. We usually lingered over dinner primarily to chat about everything from political gossip to world news.

The one thing that really bugged him was the Chinese expectation that the general manager was there to solve all staff problems, including personal. Since most of his personnel were young people, they had the typical problems of youth. They had family problems, personality problems, romantic problems, friendship problems, and every other conceivable emotional problem that one typically finds when working with young adults. And, they all came to him for guidance and assistance. He was in charge. It was his responsibility to help his staff. *Guanxi* required it. After one particularly exhausting day, his frustration overflowed. "My God, Den! I'm not running a business. I'm running a kindergarten!"

A word on interpreting is in order. It is not an easy job. The concentration required to interpret correctly is intense. Professional *simultaneous* interpreters who have been trained to United Nations standards are truly incredible. But, team rotation during lengthy speeches and negotiations, even with these professionals, is essential to addressing the mental pressure of this work.

When the interpreter is a non-professional—one who is merely bilingual and been drafted *ad hoc* into that function, the difficulties are compounded. This has to be recognized in critical cross-cultural communications. There are specific ways in which a speaker can help the interpreter get his meaning across. First, keep statements as short as possible. If a pause for interpreting comes only after a lengthy statement, there is a good chance that part of the statement will be forgotten by the interpreter. This happens more often than not. Second, avoid compound sentence structures as much as possible. Non-professional interpreters can be easily confused by multiple dependent clauses. And third, avoid idioms like the plague.

The chairman of our joint venture was a veritable fountain of Chinese idioms. He spouted them constantly—almost in every third sentence. This gave me a major headache whenever I was drafted to assist him in communicating with non-Chinese speaking executives. *Guanxi* obligations required me to acquiesce to this uncomfortable role.

The problem from my perspective was that our chairman spoke extensively in classical Chinese idioms that I did not know. Most of these idioms, called *cheng-yu* (成语) in Chinese, consisted of four, sometimes five, characters, that connoted something quite different from what they denoted. Many were derived from, or referred to, historical, literary or legendary sources. One example will suffice to demonstrate:

The idiom "judou ranji" literally means "cook the beans by burning the stalk." It connotes being injured by one's own kind. And, by extension, can refer to civil strife. The phrase itself comes from a story about Emperor Wen of the Wei dynasty (third century CE) who, desiring to kill his own brother, ordered him to compose a poem within the time it took to take seven steps—under penalty of death if he failed. The brother rapidly wrote a (very short) poem that bewailed burning the stalk to cook beans when both came from the same root. Strangely enough, the poem saved his life. The emperor had been affected by the oblique reference to their common ancestry.

Now, consider the fact that the Chinese language is replete with these idioms—each with its own background story that informs its linguistic function. Then consider that our chairman used at least one of them in every three or four sentences.

I finally complained to him, "You know, it took me four to five years to learn to read the three to four thousand characters necessary to be reasonably literate in Chinese. How can you expect me to know all these classical idiomatic expressions? You really have to cut down on their usage if you want me to help you communicate with interpreting."

His response was to give me a three-volume set of a Chinese/English dictionary of Chinese idioms that was sitting on a bookshelf in his office.

On the other hand, I've worked with many Americans whose speech was dominated by idioms—mostly sporting metaphors. Admittedly, it could be amusing to see a Chinese interpreter struggle with sentences like, "Why did the tax department move the goalposts?" or, "I thought he wouldn't get to first base on this job, but was pleasantly surprised when he knocked it out of the park." Another conversation stopper was, "That junior accountant better learn the ropes faster. He shouldn't keep those things under his hat until it's too late to call a plumber."

My favorite occurred during a complex discussion of a massive industrial project. I was with one of my all time favorite working partners, who will be introduced in the next chapter but will just be called Dave at this point, and a room full of representatives from four or five different Chinese units. The Chinese side had just made reference to a new plant technology that would make the project viable.

Dave reacted by saying," I've heard of that technology, and if it really works on industrial scale, we can really kick butt."

The Chinese interpreter looked stunned—the proverbial deer in the headlights. He then turned to me for help. Unfortunately, I was just then in the process of turning purple trying not to laugh, and to squelch a gurgle.

Dave took one look at me, and then saved the situation by saying, "Let me rephrase that."

Chapter XIII

The Environment Factor,
or
Look Before You Leap

---

*—in which a great plan and a great team make it all work in a **win-win** approach.*

I greatly enjoyed my ten years with this company. Having operations in over a hundred and fifty countries, their senior
executives were interculturally sophisticated. Including many
nationalities, they were a fascinating group of people. There is one
thing that did not occur to me when I decided to tackle a career
as a China market entry specialist. When you succeed in helping
a company get where it wants to be in China, you effectively put
yourself out of a job. After the inspection and testing joint venture
was up and running (and profitable) with some one thousand local
employees, its first general manager was rotated out of China to
another position in another subsidiary. The new general manager
was a Belgian. He was perfect for the job.

His previous position was general manager of the subsidiary in
Taiwan. He had married a local woman, and was fluent in the
Chinese language. In fact, he knew two dialects. A long-term
employee of the company, he knew the inspection business inside
out. Even better, he already had experience managing a Chinese
staff. He was the right person to take over a well-established operation in China. My services were no longer needed. It was time for
me to go.

This transition was not a happy experience for me because I had
invested a lot of intellectual and emotional capital in helping to

create, develop, and protect the China operations of my employer. Breaking that government monopoly on inspections was a very satisfying experience. In fact, it was most probably the highlight of my career. Also, I knew and liked most of the people with whom I had worked for ten years. Nevertheless, it was not difficult to find another transnational corporation who could use my help.

An American insurance company, Liberty Mutual Group, was just then in the early stages of looking at the possibility of setting up in China. Its core business was property and casualty insurance. This was of interest to me. First, I knew a little bit about the nature of their business. I had taken a course in Marine Insurance during my undergraduate days at Kings Point, and had worked for about a year as a Marine Underwriter before starting graduate studies at Penn. Also, the inspection company had a large loss adjusting division. They provided their services to property and casualty insurance companies all over the world. I had opportunity to take a look at their loss adjusting operations, including a detailed introductory tour of their divisional headquarters back in the States.

Second, the obstruction to setting up an insurance business in China was immense. As mentioned in Chapter V, the Chinese government was handing out only two business licenses each year to foreign insurance firms. This company was around eighty-ninth on the waiting list of applicants. Do the math. If that policy remained in place, their turn would come up in around forty-four years. There could be only one strategic objective: *Jump the queue!* This was a very interesting problem.

Prior to my joining their China team, the president of their international division hired a Seattle-based law firm as a consultant. This firm had set up their own representative office in Shanghai. They recommended that the insurance company also set up a representative office in that city. This was not so much a mistake *per se* as it was insufficiently considered. An *insurance* representative office was required to be set up in the municipality where they wanted to receive an insurance business license. Its only legal functions were to (1) introduce the parent company to relevant government agencies, (2) study local conditions and institutional topography of relevance to their interests, and (3) clock the requisite time, *i.e.,* two years, prior to being allowed to *apply* for a business license. And, setting up in Shanghai meant they were committed to apply for the license in Shanghai. Unfortunately, in this case, no one thought to put the words "insurance business liaison" into the Scope of Business on the representative office registration. Consequentially, that office could not serve its intended purpose. It could not run out the two-year time requirement after which the parent company would be permitted to submit an application for an insurance business license. Whereas the Seattle legal consultants had recommended the company's name be put on the roll call list, they had effectively registered on the wrong list.

Moreover, so far as I was concerned, Shanghai was not the right environment for seeking the license to operate. The vast majority of firms desirous of this license were also targeting Shanghai. Furthermore, among the companies that already had received licenses in Shanghai, one was a bitter rival of my prospective employer's firm, and that rival was hard wired into the Shanghai municipal government. They were fully capable of using their *guanxi* to obstruct a rival's progress.

I joined the small team that had been set up in Hong Kong to develop and execute a China market entry strategy. Apparently, I had been brought in to figure out how to make Shanghai work for my new employer. At that time, there were only three locations in which the Chinese government would allow foreign insurance companies to operate: Shanghai, Guangzhou and Beijing. I was uncomfortable about their precipitous move into Shanghai. Nonetheless, after ruminating over the many factors influencing market entry, a plan evolved. Shanghai would be valuable ground for establishing a unique differentiation from the other insurance companies competing for positive attention. We would be able to use this representative office as a base of operations to highlight another aspect of my new employer's business.

My new company had a great strength. They had a worker safety division that would help major business clients find ways to reduce accidents. This division was centered on an occupational safety and health (OSH) research institute that the company fully self-funded as a service to its clients. The company's OSH initiative was a valuable asset for promoting insurance.

During an indoctrination visit to this research facility, I was given an example of the kind of specialized services it provided. I was told that one of their insurance customers was a large package delivery company. Apparently, this client had been increasingly making insurance claims for knee damage to their drivers. A team of safety engineers was dispatched to investigate the reason for this statistical aberration. They discovered that the problem was a step on the driver's side of their uniformly designed trucks. Following measurements and analysis, it was determined that this step was of a size and height above the ground that increased the likelihood of getting a banged knee when mounting the cabin. The solution was a redesigned step. All the steps on their truck fleet were altered to the new design over the course of a year or so. Claims for knee injuries virtually disappeared. Everyone was a winner.

Customer loyalty was not a problem with a firm that provided such service to its clients. Customers were helped to (1) reduce worker injuries, (2) reduce staff down time, and (3) reduce insurance premiums through a better safety record. With a record like this, introducing quality OSH services that built customer loyalty was a "no-brainer" no matter which market was being developed. And so, into China we go!

Worker safety was a serious problem in China. With the rapid industrial growth of the new China, and with the massive construction work that was proceeding at a rapid pace in every metropolitan center, the problem was being exacerbated exponentially. It had reached the point where the government in Beijing decided concentrated action had to be taken, and announced an official "Year of Worker Safety" as a policy priority. Talk about perfect timing! The serendipity factor was at work. If we could become working partners with the administrative authorities that held responsibility for improving worker safety, we could establish a positive reputation in relevant governmental circles.

This was a strong possibility for the "bottom up" part of the formula that comprises the first half of an effective market entry strategy. We needed a showcase study *in China*. A bit of research revealed that the Shanghai Medical University (SMU) had a Department of Occupational Safety and Health (OSH). Their research supported OSH work under the auspices of both the Ministry of Labor and the Ministry of Public Health. One thing I learned during my time with that chemical and pharmaceutical company was that Chinese medical people are the most approachable people in the world. Accessing the department head was merely a matter of learning his name, finding his office, and knocking on the door. Professor Liang Youxin was amiable and interested in meeting the head of our OSH research institute. The net result of this approach was a cooperative program between our research institute and Shanghai Medical University.

Next, two safety engineers were added to our little team in Hong Kong, and a pilot project was designed. This program would offer our safety system evaluation services *gratis* to two local construction companies. At that time, the Pudong region of Shanghai was rapidly being transformed from farm fields into a modern metropolis. Construction covered the region with high-rise buildings, new highways, and a subway connection with the old city across the Huangpu River. This was a *target rich* environment.

Professor Liang helped us sell the idea to the Pudong Labor Bureau authorities. The latter helped us sell the idea to the construction companies. It was a difficult sell because their managers did not want to be shown to be engaged in unsafe practices on their construction sites. Nor were they keen on the idea of allowing foreigners to see their safety logs. Ultimately, negotiating a confidentiality clause into our working agreement got us over that hurdle. In actuality, we were pleasantly surprised that both of our guinea pigs, while still having something to learn about effective safety programs, had already made good efforts to ensure worker safety. Our final report on the results of our study, including a menu of recommendations for improving their safety programs, was submitted to the management of the construction companies, with copies to the Labor Bureau authorities. Evidently they liked the results because they decided to give our experimental project some publicity in the local press. We also were told that a full report on our activities and results had been sent to the Ministry of Labor and the Ministry of Construction in Beijing. Not a bad start.

Meanwhile, SMU and our safety and health research institute began a cooperative research program utilizing the former's national databases. One of them was the official Ministry of Public Health's database on occupational diseases linked to industrial demographics. The other served the Ministry of Labor with a database on occupational injuries. SMU's resources would enable our researchers to access an extensive body of information, with the objective of generating peer-reviewed papers in appropriate scientific journals.

While this probably doesn't sound very interesting to someone not in this field, our efforts made it easy for us to access the ministry level bureaucrats responsible for occupational safety and health (OSH). The Ministry of Labor had an OSH Bureau, a Bureau of Occupational Safety Management, and a Bureau of Mine Safety and Health Inspection. It also ran China's National Institute for OSH. The Ministry of Public Health had several departments for disease prevention and health inspection. They also ran an Industrial Hygiene Laboratory and the National Institute of Radiation Hygiene Protection and Monitoring. And then there were safety supervision departments in all the many and various industrial ministries, including those for construction, power generation, coal mining, machine building, metallurgy, chemicals, railways, etc.

Our institutional map-making uncovered another useful element in the mix. The State Bureau of Technical Supervision (old friends from my days with the inspection and testing company) had the job of promulgating OHS standards. As such, they worked with the researchers and laboratories in all these safety and health supervision units. SBTS was happy to assist with introductions and guidance as we traversed this bureaucratic maze. It's nice to have friends in the right place at the right time. At the same time, SBTS welcomed the opportunity to align with a strong, positive initiative that enhanced their own reputation. *Guanxi* was at work again.

Of course, one of the characteristics of Chinese bureaucracy is that the plethora of administrations, bureaus, departments, and divisions rarely coordinate their respective activities with other units. All of these many units had parallel and overlapping responsibilities for worker safety, but the lack of communications among them was distinctly noticeable. Our involvement resulted in our becoming a conduit for sharing information and ideas among these various governmental organizations. Other companies in other industries have found themselves in a similar role as they worked between and among various strictly vertical bureaucratic structures. Eventually, an attempt was made by the central government to gather a number of the ministerial safety departments into a single worker safety bureau. We never knew for certain if our efforts to coordinate their work had some influence in the making of that decision, although we liked to think so.

Without going into all the details, suffice it to say that cooperative activities with these units in Beijing took a great deal of effort. Each unit had its own unique needs, agendas, and mode of operations. By addressing their particular concerns with as much professional assistance as possible, our corporate image on the ministerial level became quite positive. We were seen as a unique insurance company in that we had much to offer in support of some of the government's industrial objectives. This gave us a strategic springboard for *jumping the queue*. Now we had to decide on the best placement for that springboard. We had to dive into the right spot for the best swimming. That is when I recalled Chongqing.

About three or four years before I joined the insurance company, one of China's state councilors (I forget which one) visited Hong Kong and made a public appearance. The local newspapers reported that his message was a plea that foreign businesses consider investing in the western regions of China. His concern was the growing disparity in economic development between the rich coastal regions and the economically depressed western hinterland. At that time, he specifically referred to the large interior city of Chongqing as the "Gateway to the West," and suggested that this metropolis was the best place to start looking at potential investments. (Chongqing is located around 1,500 km up the Yangzi River from Shanghai.) By the time we were thrashing about in search of a viable strategy for *jumping the queue,* the concern about attracting investment to Chongqing and China's western provinces had evolved into an official policy of the central government. This was dynamically demonstrated when Chongqing was elevated to a direct-reporting municipality—a kind of federal district, similar in status to Beijing, Shanghai, and Tianjin. A municipality with a population of thirty-one million was about to undergo major changes in infrastructure, industry, and construction.

The expansion of the locks at the Three Gorges Dam would

improve waterway access to Chongqing as the "head of naviga-tion" on the Yangzi River. Eventually, this major artery would carry one-third of China's inland and coastal waterborne freight. Also, plans were now underway to make Chongqing, already an industrial center, a major hub for both rail and highway transport. It seemed to me that Chongqing would eventually become China's Chicago, a major distribution center for the hinterland.

Our institutional mapping of the agencies and organizations relevant to the approval process (both formal and informal) for an insurance license application led to another interesting discov-ery. The leaders of the State Planning Commission, a powerful, policy-making body that held the purse strings of governmental planning, had close professional and personal links to the gov-ernmental leaders of Chongqing. The official policy of funneling economic development through Chongqing to the western regions came straight out of this commission. We had found an effective target for the "top down" part of the strategic mix.

Not only was it a good guess that Chongqing might be the next major metropolis to open up to foreign insurance companies, but also our growing reputation as a substantive contributor to China's concerns about worker safety could serve as a catalyst for such lib-eralization. Spring boarding on our increasingly multifaceted OSH program, we put an effective communications plan together. This plan enabled us to connect with the State Planning Commission to ask for an introduction to their counterparts in Chongqing. They were happy to oblige. What we had to offer dovetailed with their own strategic objectives.

Some of these various state commission and ministerial con-nections that we were making in Beijing facilitated our becoming acquainted with the leadership in China's insurance administration. These introductory visits began with the Peoples Insurance Com-pany of China (PICC), which had held an insurance monopoly in China until 1988. At that time, a handful of other state-owned entities was authorized to open insurance operations. These visits extended to the China Insurance Regulatory Commission (CIRC) after it was established by the central government in 1998.

Our objective here was to enable our own senior insurance executives to engage in an ongoing, low-key professional dialogue that would slowly establish our qualifications and credentials in this specialized field. This was an important part of our overall strategy because the people in these two organizations would play a critical role in the approval process when we eventually reached the point of submitting an application for an insurance business license.

By riding the slowly expanding wave of interest in Chongqing, a wide-ranging program of cooperative activities with Chongqing's municipal leaders and economic development authorities was constructed. Technical exchanges were initiated with worker safety and workers' compensation insurance as topics. An Insurance Representative Office, with a small staff of locally hired people, was registered in Chongqing. These moves gave substance to senior executive visits to Beijing and Chongqing.

On one of these visits, the mayor of Chongqing asked our chairman and CEO if he would consider looking at government-approved projects in Chongqing to see if any might be able to attract foreign investment. Our chairman gave exactly the right answer. He said that he would direct one of our investment units to start an investigation into that possibility. He clarified that this team would report to him if they identified a viable project that met our established criteria for making an investment. He went on to explain that the exploration process is a matter of exercising *due diligence* to fully understand the potential for both risks and returns on investment, and to identify the kind of adjustments that might be needed to make a development project viable for potential investors. This promise was kept. A San Francisco-based investment subsidiary was instructed to explore potential investment projects in Chongqing. Shortly thereafter, a conference in Chongqing was arranged in which the invited speakers presented papers on how investments were considered, and what standards applied for decision-making on potential investment projects.

It was around this time that I transferred to this investment unit. The subsidiary president, A. David Dickert, had invited me to join his team after I had assisted him during his first forays into China. This was a whole new experience for me. Dickert had started his career as a chemical engineer in various Fortune 500 companies. Then, with an MBA under his belt, he joined Rohm and Haas in new product development, working up into mergers and acquisitions, ending up as president and CEO of a wholly owned oil and gas exploration subsidiary. From there, he started his own oil and gas exploration outfit, eventually selling it to a Wall Street investment group. He was the right man to look at the potential of new industrial enterprises, weeding out the unfeasible and absurd. I provided insight into the Chinese side of the equation—facilitating whatever had to be done with intelligence gathering and relationship building. We became in essence a two-man due diligence and project development team, each with differing but complementary skills and knowledge. Our *modus operandi* was a combination of focused hard work and much laughter.

The Chinese government clearly took this portion of our group's commitment to Chongqing seriously. Our investment unit negotiated a letter-of-intent that set out the general terms of our cooperation with Chongqing Municipality's planning department. This would facilitate our access to people and information for our project research and due diligence work. When our senior executives agreed to have the formal signing in the group's headquarters in the States, we were advised that the party secretary of the Chongqing Municipal Government would head their delegation to witness the signing. The party secretary is the top guy in any governmental unit. That was an extremely strong signal of interest.

The role of our investment unit was to examine in depth development projects that had been approved by Chongqing's planning department. Primarily a *due diligence* function, our investigations had to come up with reliable, verifiable information about these various projects. This included not just the financial data, but also engineering design, market conditions, management structure, production technology, regulatory environment, and anything else pertinent to project viability.

The most interesting project idea for me was the possibility of establishing a joint-venture tug-and-barge operation on the Yangzi River, including offshore cargo shipping in East Asian waters, with a Chongqing-based firm. The Three Gorges Dam project included the construction of a new set of locks that would allow larger barges with greater carrying capacity to reach Chongqing. And, the Chinese transportation authorities in Beijing were, at that time, looking seriously at a variety of policies that would stimulate improved infrastructure and freight traffic on the Yangzi. At the time of this writing, over 30 percent of China's river, canal and coastwise freight moved on the Yangzi.

The Chongqing river freight firm had been given the okay to look for a foreign partner. We decided our part was to escort the potential Chinese partner to American shipping companies with similar commercial and technical capabilities to see if we could generate interest in such a project. If we could find a partner with the appropriate experience and technology to enhance the assets and operations of the proposed Chinese partner, we could have a viable investment project to submit to our executive board for review.

On one such visit in Houston, our entourage included the captain of a Yangzi River tugboat. He was fascinated with the computerized control room of the American barge line in which all the company's vessels were tracked minute-by-minute on a giant screen. The system had instant direct voice communication with any of their tug captains, as their vast fleet moved purpose-fully throughout America's inland waterways. He was completely flabbergasted by the gift presented to him by one of the American tug captains, who gave him a copy of the thick book of Mississippi River navigation charts. When he found his voice again, he said, "Are you sure it's okay for you to do this? If I gave anyone copies of our Yangzi River charts, I would be arrested for violating our state secrets regulations." We assured him that the publication of nautical charts was a government function, and anyone could buy them for commercial or recreational purposes.

Ultimately, this project didn't get off the ground for a num-ber of reasons. The timing was not right for the three American tug-and-barge lines we had approached. Their various business development resources were all heavily engaged elsewhere at that time. Nevertheless, we had put a great deal of time, effort, and money in trying to make this project happen, and the Chongqing authorities responsible for economic planning and development appreciated our work. They were also aware that our coopera-tive effort exposed the managers of their river transport company to new knowledge about relevant technology and operational management.

I must confess that I would have seriously considered deferring my impending retirement if this project had come to fruition. After all, I was a Kings Pointer—how could I resist the opportunity to be involved with running freight along one of the great rivers of the world.

Sometimes we were asked to look into a project that looked worse the more we examined it. We then had to create an exit strategy that would diplomatically lead the Chinese to decide to go back to the drawing board. The best tactic in this situation was to help the Chinese understand what problems had to be solved in order for a specific project to be commercially viable.

One such project came from the China National Petroleum and

Natural Gas Corporation, often referred to as PetroChina. This company was a large, state-owned oil and gas exploration and development unit. With headquarters based in Beijing, they had an operational presence in the Sichuan-Chongqing region due to the natural gas fields located there. A number of projects were brewing that revolved about natural gas usage. For example, the municipal government wanted to set up filling stations throughout Chongqing to fuel a fleet of busses and taxis with compressed natural gas. However, before that enterprise could be considered, they had to develop an economical plant to convert their natural gas into a usable vehicular fuel.

PetroChina had commenced discussions with an American oil and gas exploration company that was already operating in the South China Sea. I'm not sure how Dickert was pulled into the mix, but as the representative of an investment and project evaluation group already exploring the Chongqing market, and given his background in the oil and gas industry, he was a logical choice. While Dave listened intently to the project details in terms of technology and financing, I tried to sort out the plethora of participating Chinese units and their respective agendas.

In addition to PetroChina's head office representatives, including their chief economist, but mostly business planning and refining technology research people, there were operational types from their offices in Chengdu in Sichuan Province and in Chongqing. There were also delegations from the Chongqing Chemical Industry Bureau, the Sichuan Petroleum Industry Bureau, the China Huanqiu Chemical Engineering Corporation (based in Beijing), the Chongqing Planning Commission, the Chongqing Gas Corporation, the Chongqing Municipal Government Foreign Affairs Office, and a few more whose business cards seem to have been lost from my files. But you get the idea. We needed a rather large conference room for these discussions.

This was one of those classically inoperable situations that can happen in China. Each unit represented in the room had differing concerns, ideas, interests, and agendas. It was virtually impossible to sort out who were decision-influencers and who were decision-makers. Even worse, the players often changed from one meeting to the next. Furthermore, the situation did not allow for the time it takes for individuals to develop comfortable personal relationships outside of the meetings, which sometimes took place in Beijing and sometimes in Chongqing. I told Dave that sorting out the various agendas was going to be tough, if not impossible, under the circumstances. To me, it was a virtual nightmare.

The technology research people from PetroChina and China Huanqiu Chemical Engineering believed that the technology they needed to make the project viable was already in existence. They pointed to specific projects in several countries around the globe where it was in use. Dickert confided to me that he was pretty sure they did not have correct information. Saying nothing in the meeting, he later phoned an old friend in London for a chat. He then asked him to pack a bag and hop a flight to China. Dickert said he would cover all costs and the usual consulting fee.

When his friend arrived, Dave briefed him on the situation. At our next meeting on this project, Dave introduced his friend as the project manager who had been in charge of developing the various facilities around the world to which the Chinese had referred as proof that the requisite technology was already in operation. Documentary proof was presented for review. Then, our consulting engineer stated, "All those projects were pilot projects, and none of them have yet proved commercially viable for upgrading to an industrial scale. Furthermore, it's going to take several more years, at least, to get to that point." That basically ended the discussion.

Dave's final comment to me on this project was, "Sometimes you have to spend a little money to ensure you don't waste a lot of money on nonsense." I applauded his "diplomatic" solution.

Around this time, the Chongqing Municipal Development

Planning Commission asked us how to go about attracting investment in two large wastewater treatment plants that were already under construction. These projects were needed because of the Three Gorges Dam, being built downstream from the city. The dam would turn the fast moving waters of the upper Yangzi into a large, deep, slow moving reservoir. Without a new and massive wastewater treatment system for the municipality, the entire upper river would be turned into a huge cesspool.

Linking up with an engineering design firm that was already working in Chongqing and Shanghai, we helped the Chongqing authorities process an application to the U.S. Trade and Development Agency for a grant to fund a financial feasibility study. We then carried out a joint investigation of both the technological and financial aspects of these projects. One of the study's primary objectives was to determine if the fiscal aspects of the plants when in operation would be able to provide a reasonable return on capital investment. My working partner in this exercise, Jamil Sopher, had been brought on board because of his knowledge and experience with financial analysis of major projects in developing countries during his lengthy tenure at the World Bank. He was another great working partner who became a valued friend. The analysis uncovered problems and complications that we hoped would help the Chongqing Commission to reexamine their project management. We also determined that while the project was feasible from an engineering perspective, we found that the financial structure planned by the Chinese, based on metered potable water usage, was problematical. Simply put, their intended structure would not provide a reasonable rate of return for participants in the investment. Our final report recommended a different financing model that we believed to be viable, but it was not adopted by the Chongqing authorities for the new wastewater treatment plants. However, I understand that they later used our recommendation on another development project.

In addition to examining these and other potential investment projects, our company demonstrated a commitment to the municipality by funding the construction of a new elementary school in an economically challenged rural locale outside the metropolitan area. We also accepted various invitations to participate in local colloquia speaking engagements at the local university, local industrial expositions, and government-sponsored ceremonies. For example, when the Three Gorges Dam project management organized a ribbon-cutting ceremony at the dam site, because of the international controversy over the needs of China's power grid vs. environmental risks stimulated by this project, representatives from only seven transnational corporations showed up for the ceremony. We were one of the seven.

The net result of this multiplicity of involvements, giving the municipal authorities opportunity to see various facets of our company in action, was a successful conclusion to our strategy. Eventually, they told us an exact date when we should submit our application for an insurance business license. At the same time, they advised that the central government would soon announce that Chongqing would be opened up to foreign insurance companies. They confided to us that our license would be issued on the day immediately following that announcement. We had successfully *jumped the queue.*

This achievement was built on a foundation created by reading the political environment correctly. In a country under one-party control, supporting policies that match your interests and capabilities, your mission and objectives, is an effective way to establish your reputation and credentials. China's increasing awareness of the importance of occupational safety to economic and social welfare allowed us to showcase our company's expertise in this area. Responding positively to China's desire to bring transnational businesses to Chongqing allowed us to partner with government authorities who would support our business objectives.

There was another vital element in this success. Everyone involved with the execution of our strategic plan, from corporate chairman to field staff, understood the overall vision. Each and every team member knew how his role was a part of the whole. Yes, corporate internal conflicts created a few speed bumps, but they were minor distractions for the most part. This speaks well of the company's internal communications as the multiple tactical situations were managed by a variety of team members.

All-in-all, very satisfying.

AFTERWORD

My years in China covered the period in which America's leaders instituted the policy of engagement with the Chinese. The objective of this policy was to encourage the Chinese to come out of their ideological shell and join the family of nations. Serving on the front lines of this cross-cultural effort gave me an exciting and absorbing career. It was a continuous learning experience. It also provided much satisfaction in being able to contribute materially to creating cooperative relationships where all the individuals involved had the opportunity to grow in intercultural competence.

The *engagement* policy has clearly been a success. China is now inextricably involved on the world stage—politically, economically, and socially. They are at once both competitors and cooperators. They have their own interests and concerns. Their perspectives on many issues of common interest are different from ours. However, they have also learned to appreciate the Western "can do" approach to problem solving.

On a personal level, I have liked most of the Chinese with whom I have worked. Yes, I've met a couple of real stinkers here and there. But you'll find that in any society anywhere. Like people the world over, the Chinese are all individuals, complete with personalities, agendas, hopes, and dreams.

Collectively, the Chinese perceive that their civilization was one of the largest and most powerful in the world for over three thousand years. Some of their imperial dynasties provided their people with periods of relative peace and prosperity lasting longer than the entire history of the United States. They see their relative weakness during the couple of hundred years of the Industrial Revolution in the West as an historical aberration. What they are doing now is restoring what they consider their rightful place in the scheme of things in this world. They want the "face" of China to be respected.

Despite what the isolationists and closet imperialists in the American political arena may say, the nation of China does not have to be an enemy. There is no place for the mythology of the *Yellow Peril* in the twenty-first century. If my experiences show anything, they suggest that it is possible to find a fundamental harmony in our relationships with the Chinese people, even if it takes a bit of negotiation and compromise.

At the risk of seeming facile, I would say that the *Confucian* principle of harmony, based on mutual respect, provides a foundation for intercultural connections. Nevertheless, it is worth being mindful of the strategic principles of *Sun Zi* when negotiating a working relationship. Idealistic ends still require realistic means. And yet, this applies to market entry and problem solving throughout the globe. On a more personal level, it boiled down to my having so darn much fun and growth through my experiences in the Chinese part of the world.

But I never wrote to thank my seventh grade geography teacher.

ABOUT THE AUTHOR

An ex-merchant mariner, **Den Leventhal** spring-boarded from graduate work in Asian studies at the University of Pennsylvania and National Taiwan University to a thirty-year career as a China market entry strategist. Competent in Chinese (Mandarin), his work has taken him to sixty-two Chinese cities, interacting with a wide range of Chinese people from ministers of state to factory workers.

A native Pennsylvanian, Leventhal has always enjoyed exploring the world around him. But it was as a graduate of the United States Merchant Marine Academy and an officer on ocean-going commercial vessels that his fascination and interest in East Asia grew. Business opportunities drew him into a world of navigating culture and corporate needs as world economics became more interconnected. Recognizing the importance of intercultural competency, Leventhal has kept a foot in both academia and economic growth as an explorer, negotiator, educator, and trouble shooter.

Leventhal spearheaded the creation of two successful Chinese-foreign joint ventures, and managed due diligence, institutional mapping, cross-cultural relationships, staff development, government affairs, market entry strategies, marketing and purchasing activities throughout China during his quarter-century residence in East Asia. Currently residing on the banks of a Maryland Eastern Shore river with his wife Mary, Leventhal messes about in boats when he is not busy with writing, music, archery, or his volunteer work with the Natural Resources Police and in local schools.